CHANGING ME FROM THE INSIDE OUT

Changing Me from the Inside Out

Printed in the United States of America
ISBN 978-1-946425-35-5

Book Design by CSinclaire Write-Design
Book Cover by Klevur

Write Way Publishing Company

Other Books by Patti Fralix

A Year in the Life of a Recovering Spendaholic

Follow the author as she journals her commitment not to purchase anything non-disposable for an entire year to change her "spendaholic" behaviors. The stimulus for this book was a trip to New Orleans soon after Hurricane Katrina, seeing the devasting loss, and coming to terms with what is important in life.

How to Thrive in Spite of Mess, Stress, and Less (Second Edition)

You will find relatable, personable, and helpful guidance in simple steps about discovering your passion, converting your passion to action, and defining and living a truly prosperous life.

Dedication

I dedicate this book and its memories first of all to my wonderful family: my dear husband, Mike, our daughters Tara and Chatham and their families, my cousin Paula and her family, and dear friend MoMo, who is more family than friend. While Mike and I were on St. Maarten during Hurricane Irma, our family was in Raleigh, worrying about us and praying for us. We also had family and friends all over the world who through Facebook and other means, reached out to us and our family expressing love and hope. To all who suffered through this with us, we give our deepest gratitude. To our daughter Tara who spent many hours working on getting us home, especially with American Airlines, you are your mother's daughter! To daughters Tara and Chatham and granddaughters Mary Grace, Elsie, and Virginia, seeing all of you at the airport when we arrived home will always be one of my most treasured memories. To grandson, Drew, who brought more happiness into our lives with his arrival in 2018.

This book is also dedicated to Rivka, my life coach who taught me how to live through change, becoming better in the process. My work on this is not done yet, but I am better because of Rivka.

Finally, this book is dedicated to Lee Heinrich, who believed I had this book in me and gently pushed me to complete it in a timely manner. I will always be grateful for Lee's influence in my life.

CHANGING ME FROM THE INSIDE OUT

My Hurricane Irma Experience on St. Maarten and Other Life Changing Events

Patti Fralix

Write Way Publishing

Table of Contents

Introduction

2017 was quite the year for me. It was one scary event after another. This cycle culminated in living through the strongest hurricane on record—Hurricane Irma, a category 5 hurricane when it came ashore on St. Maarten where my husband, Mike, and I were vacationing. I pride myself on my resiliency, but I must confess that cumulative events of that year threw me off center. I have talked about and taught about *change* for twenty-five years. I published a book in 2002 about dealing with the mess and stress that life throws at us, and sixteen years later in 2018, I published a second edition of that book—while still processing all the mess and stress that had happened to me during 2017.

For the past twenty-five years of speaking, consulting, and coaching on many different topics, one of the most common subject areas of my business has been change. I have often used Gandhi's quote, "You must be the change you wish to see in the world." I have always believed that there must be consistency between what we say and who we are, for if not, we are talking our walk, not walking our talk. Our audiences and customers can see right through that duplicity and will find us inauthentic. Those of us who want to change things for the better have to spend as much time on ourselves as on teaching our subject matter!

I am a work in process as I try to assimilate the lessons my life continues to offer me about change. My 2017 cycle of change lessons started on March 7 when I had a car accident that seriously injured my left leg. Perhaps even more significantly, it created in me a fear of driving. That was something I had never before experienced.

I had left a meeting in downtown Raleigh, North Carolina, and was headed to a meeting in Cary. It had been an almost perfect day. (More about the "almost perfect day" later.) I had attended a luncheon meeting at City Club Raleigh, then spent an hour catching up on some work before leaving to attend another meeting about thirty minutes away in Cary.

I was midway between downtown Raleigh and Cary when all of a sudden, I realized that the car in front of me was stopping or stopped. Even more than a year later, I still do not know why that car in front of me didn't come into my awareness until there was insufficient time to safely slow down or stop. An accident occurred.

I have thought about this many times. To my knowledge,

I was not distracted. I think that I was driving between forty-five and fifty miles an hour, which was the speed limit in that area. All I knew at the time, and still all I know, is that all of a sudden, I realized that I had to slow down or stop, and there did not seem to be sufficient time to do either.

The next thing I knew, I had hit the car in front of me, had come to an abrupt stop, and the air bags had deployed. After a few minutes or seconds, I realized that I was okay. There was no obvious damage to me other than I was shaken. I realized that my car was stopped in the middle of a busy highway, which was not a safe place to be. I decided that I needed to get me and, if possible, my car out of the middle of the road. I looked around, and amazingly, there were no other cars in the immediate area at that exact moment. What happened next was one of my most frightening experiences.

I opened my car door, planning to get out, and all of a sudden, my car started moving. I was thrown onto the pavement, and my leg was pinned under my left tire. My car continued to roll backwards. I remember thinking that I could die right there, that I might not be able to extricate myself from under the tire. The thought flashed through my mind that I had to help myself, even if I died trying to live. So, I tried to move my pinned leg. I did not feel any pain. This was amazing to me later when I saw the condition of my leg.

After what seemed like forever, and I do not know if my actions had anything to do with it, my car rolled a bit more, and the tire rolled off of my leg. Once freed from the tire, I managed to get up and move to the side of the road. Almost immediately, a young woman came over to me and asked if I was all right. She began to help me. I was not all right, but I was well aware that I was glad to be alive.

The woman who helped me told me that my van had backed into her (new) car before it finally came to a stop. She said, "Do not worry one minute about my car. Let's make sure that you are taken care of." She stayed with me until others arrived. I will always remember her kindness.

I did not see what happened to the car in front of me that I hit from behind, and no one from that car came to see how I was. It did not appear that anyone was injured in that vehicle. I am curious about that. What was it that made one person be concerned about a stranger and not about her damaged car, and another person, in a similar situation, not even come back to see if there were any injuries from that accident? I have some thoughts about that, but they would just be assumptions, so I will not mention them.

Soon thereafter, the rescue squad arrived and took me to the emergency room for treatment.

I was there for eight hours then discharged. I recovered at home for two weeks before I was able to put weight on my leg to walk. My good friend Maureen, a nurse practitioner, took care of me, changing my dressings and making sure that healing occurred as expected. My husband, Mike, was beside me all of that time for which I was thankful.

I was quite shaken from that accident and did not want to drive, although I knew that I would eventually have to. My van was totaled, but I was in no hurry to get another vehicle. It was a month after the accident before I drove again and three months before we purchased another van for me. I had two requirements for that purchase. I insisted on a recent model, one with all of the "new" safety features, and I did not want the same model that I had totaled. Too many scary memories now for that van.

After I was physically able to drive again and had my new van, it was not long until I had another car accident. While this one was not as serious as the first, the accident was once again my fault, and it increased my fear of driving. I joked more than once—maybe not entirely without some seriousness—about needing to find a chauffeur.

This second moving vehicle accident was minor, although the cost to repair the other car and mine wasn't. I sideswiped that car when I miscalculated making a turn. No one was hurt, thankfully, but my new van was no longer pristine.

Then in late August, a third car event occurred. A friend and I were in Nashville, Tennessee, heading back to Birmingham, Alabama, for me to catch a flight home. We left Nashville a little later than we should have for a leisurely drive to Birmingham and then got caught in early morning traffic. After getting through the worst of the traffic, we looked forward to a more peaceful drive, but all of a sudden, something flew off of a truck in front of us. My friend Judy, who was driving, had no time to avoid the debris. We hit it, and immediately her car tire flattened. She slowed down and pulled off the road. The truck driver pulled off the road too, checked his load, jumped back in his truck, and sped off, leaving us in the dust. I took a picture of his license plate with my phone, but it was not clear enough to read.

After a few minutes of sitting on the side of the road and calming ourselves down, I called AAA to request their help in changing our tire. I have been glad more than once in the past few years that I have AAA. It is comforting to know that as a member of AAA help is at hand regardless of what car I am in or where I am.

We waited in the car on the side of the road for the AAA person to arrive. He arrived in less than an hour, changed our tire, and we were again on our way. It was obvious that given this delay, I would miss my flight from Birmingham to Raleigh, but I was not concerned about that. I was just glad we were safe. We were so grateful that we were not hurt and relieved that car tires are easily replaced or repaired, but with this being my third negative event in a moving vehicle in a short period of time, I was rattled to say the least.

So now you know my trifecta of automobile mishaps that started the very odd, and several times scary, string of events I experienced in 2017. But I have told you about these events for a reason that goes back to the core of my work: change—what to do with it when it happens. And that leads me back for a moment to my earlier comment about having had "an almost perfect day" right before my first vehicle accident.

When I arrived at City Club Raleigh for the luncheon, I parallel parked on Fayetteville Street. I got out of the van and went around to the right side of the vehicle to pay the meter. The meter was across from my right front tire, and I noticed that I had parked too close to the curb; my tire was into the curb. I decided to move the tire off of the curb and went around to the driver's side of the van. I did not plan to start the car, just turn the wheel enough to move the tire from the curb. I opened the door, leaned into the car, and turned the wheel. The van began to roll backwards! I immediately put my foot on the brake, and the van stopped rolling. I didn't pay particular attention to this as I was focused on getting to my lunch meeting. It was only later that I would recall the van starting to roll backwards when, to the best of my memory, I had not even turned on the ignition. This little event was a *discontinuity* that may have repeated itself in my serious car accident that occurred later that day when my van rolled backwards and briefly pinned my leg after the van had been fully stopped.

I recall exactly when I first heard the word "discontinuity" and understood its meaning. It was when I attended a fellowship program at Wharton in 1993. Discontinuity is defined as "a gap, a break, something that isn't continuous." In essence, a discontinuity is something that doesn't fit, something out of the norm of what you should expect.

At the time I was in the Wharton Fellowship program, I was still employed as Vice President at Rex Hospital, a position from which I had technically been terminated, and was working out a severance. When discontinuities were discussed in my studies at Wharton, I was able to recall situations that fit into the discontinuity category in my position at Rex. At the time they were occurring, I did not notice them or understand the meaning of what was happening.

As I look back, one reason for this obliviousness no doubt was that I was so strong-willed that I thought I could survive the political problems that were threatening my job. I was competent, but it wasn't about competence. I was confident, to the point of being arrogant, that I could "fix it," but that could not save my job. I was committed, but commitment was not enough. The one in power had decided that I needed to go. That was what it was about. Had I paid enough attention, early enough, had I "read the tea leaves" accurately, my departure might have been smoother for me and the organization.

Another variable that is often involved when discontinuities occur is the failure to accept change quickly enough. Life provides most of us many opportunities to deal with change that we do not want and did not seek, and we have the choice to move with the change or resist it. My personality and my life circumstances have too often found me resisting change too long for my own good. The fact that I teach others how to deal with change better than I sometimes deal with change myself is interesting, but not unexpected. Often we teach what *we* need to learn!

It turns out that the three car accidents within months were only a prelude for a truly epic-for-me event—experiencing Hurricane Irma in all her power on St. Maarten in September 2017. I'm not getting any younger, and I never want to rush time, but I was still glad to see the end of 2017 and to have lived through it. I finished that year in a spirit of self-evaluation, and I have spent 2018 learning to deal with the lessons these events brought to me. The analysis is ongoing and evolving. I know it has not yet all unfolded. I did and do realize that I need to deal with the changes that occurred, find the meaning in them, and make some changes in my life as a result of the life-changing events.

While I have to say it was not so for Mike, my own experience with Hurricane Irma was life changing for me. I think that would have been true even without the car events/accidents that had occurred a few months before Irma. But having so many problems happen so close together, then Hurricane Irma—well, I believe that things happen for a reason. I wanted to try to figure out the reason for the challenges of my 2017 cycle.

Dealing with change, especially change outside of our control, is never easy. While my car accidents were my fault, the debris from the truck that flattened my friend's car tire and the chaos of Hurricane Irma were not. But regardless of fault, I did and do believe that my own experiences in these events were to teach me something. It is my responsibility to learn the lessons.

It is important and necessary to say first and foremost

that while my Hurricane Irma experience was traumatic for me, many, many other people on St. Maarten, both the Dutch side and the French side, as well as in other locations suffered so very much more than I did from Irma and from other hurricanes and natural and man-made disasters. I am very conscious of that and do not compare my experience to theirs.

Lives, homes, businesses, and property were all lost in Hurricane Irma. Lives were irreparably changed, I'm sure, in many cases. Many people have had to start all over again—from nothing. The island of Barbuda was almost entirely destroyed by Irma, and the north coast of Cuba also suffered badly. Richard Branson's Necker Island suffered a direct hit and was devastated. Tortola also had significant damage from that storm.

While Irma only grazed Puerto Rico, Hurricane Maria made landfall there as a category 4 hurricane on September 20, 2017, causing damage that the U.S. territory has yet to recover from more than one year later. Some U.S. citizens have expressed concern that a U.S. territory did not receive more aid and assistance from the U.S. I will leave that for others to debate.

There are stories to tell in all these events, but they are not mine to tell. Mike and I were able to return to our family and to our home in Raleigh. Many others lost their home and all of their possessions. We were and are fortunate. I am aware of and respectful of all these facts. My experience is all I can record here. I know it could have been so much worse.

This book is not just about my four life-changing events in 2017. It is not just about Hurricane Irma. It is more about the *effect* of the accidents and the storm. This book is really about change, including change that happens outside of our control. We all experience change frequently—sometimes it's change we initiate or invite, sometimes it's some change that is outside of our control. How we respond or react to these changes directly impacts us through the lessons they teach us. In some cases, our responses can even significantly impact the direction of our life and the lives of those around us.

I have taught for years that personality, self-esteem, and confidence are always involved in how we deal with change. Age and life circumstances are also factors, and healthy personal relationships make us better able to deal with life in general. Dealing with change is a mixed bag of emotions, skills, and preparedness.

As I have examined change factors in my work over the years, I have considered whether there is a relationship between gender and how a person deals with change. I believe there is. In general, many women have been socialized to be somewhat dependent and interdependent, while many men have been socialized to be independent. Recent years have seen this socialization process begin to change in American society—though perhaps not to the degree we expect or hope.

This is not a major premise of this book, so I will not discuss this shift in any detail. And I am prepared to be proven wrong! I mention this factor only in support of my statements that Mike "accepted" the experience of Hurricane Irma very differently than I did.

For Mike, Irma was an adventure, although he was aware of its seriousness. He never thought we would die, and I definitely thought we could or even would. I do not know what accounted for our differing perceptions of this event. We were together through the whole storm. I have to say, Mike has experienced several other serious weather events. He was in Cancun during Hurricane Wilma and in Haiti during the earthquake. He was also in Tokyo, Honduras, and California during earthquakes! Some people have said they do not want to travel where Mike goes, to which Mike has responded, "Why not? I have always arrived home safely!" I should have remembered that during Irma!

So, here I am, writing my account and sharing my thoughts, writing "I" rather more frequently than "we" in some parts because of our "different" shared experience.

This book is divided into four parts. Part I begins before Irma and even travels back before the other life-changing events of 2017. Part II is our time during Irma and our evacuation to return home. It is also about St. Maarten one year after Irma. Most of all, this book is about *change*, *lessons learned*, and *gratitude* found in Part III. Part IV is really a call to action about dealing with change and a brief look at three simple tools I use in my business that might help you consider the way you deal with change.

May you never experience a life-threatening event. Well,

here's a better wish for you. If and when you experience a *life-changing event*, which we all do, even if it is not a *life-threatening event*, may it change you into your best self. Only then can you live your best life.

PART I

Before the Storm

Our St. Maarten Beginning

Mike and I, and for most years, family and friends, have been travelling to St. Maarten each year since 2000. It all began in December of that year.

I had never been to the Caribbean, and Mike had only been to Puerto Rico, so we decided to go for a week that year in the middle of December. We traded one of our time share properties and travelled to St. Maarten, staying at the Royal Islander Club La Plage for a week. I do not remember what we did that week, other than relax, eat wonderful food, and shop. Eighteen years later, I still enjoy all of those things.

We loved the island from the beginning, though I don't

think either of us can pin down specific reasons why. We just do. It certainly has to do with the beauty of the island and the friendliness of the people. The island has two distinct areas, St. Martin, the French side, and St. Maarten, the Dutch side. One of the facts the locals are proudest of is that these two countries have been living on the same island peacefully for more than three hundred years.

The food on the island is considered to be some of the best in the Caribbean, and one area, Grand Case, is considered the Caribbean gourmet capital. The water is beautiful, and with 37 beaches, there is plenty to do and see. The shopping is wonderful too. Still, there are other areas that can boast most of the same things. We just have an affinity for St. Maarten and have not spent too much time trying to figure out why. It has become part of our lives.

On our last vacation day on St. Maarten in 2000, Mike and I were relaxing at the pool when one of the sales people came by and asked if we wanted to see something to purchase. Not planning to do anything but look, we said, "Sure." Mike and I like space—even when it is only the two of us—so the agent began by showing us some lovely, spacious units. At that point, I don't know if we were really serious prospective buyers or curious guests, but when we saw a three-bedroom penthouse that would be perfect for our family, we became prospective buyers.

The unit was beautiful, the kitchen well-equipped, and

the ocean front location alone could have sold the property to us. But best of all, there was a huge wrap around deck that we could see through the lovely windows. All that was left to lock down was our two-week ownership. Our weeks became the end of August and early September. That was fine with us although we knew it was hurricane season. It would be seventeen years before hurricane season became much of a problem for us.

2017 — The Week before Irma Arrived

August 26 was the start of our 2017 two-week vacation in St. Maarten. As usual, we arrived on Saturday, and the first thing we did was head down to the pool to say hello to the staff.

The mood was a little different this year. We were not there long before it became obvious that the staff was worried. There was a hurricane out in the Atlantic that was strengthening, and some of the models predicted dire conditions for St. Maarten. Thinking back now, I cannot remember knowing of the hurricane threat before making our trip, or at least, I was not aware that the threat was serious.

In our seventeen years of visiting St. Maarten, there have been a few years that we have had hurricane conditions, but nothing serious. A couple of years, we have been boarded up for a day, and conditions did not return to normal for a couple of more days, but those were more tropical storms that could become low level hurricanes. We were more inconvenienced than frightened.

It was still too early to tell what the hurricane would actually do, but as we travelled around the island the next few days, many of the people of the island were obviously very worried. There was much talk of the two hurricane models, the European model and the American model. Mike and I did a lot of listening, not yet concerned enough to consider not staying on the island. We did not even talk about our options much in the first few days. We just went about our usual vacation activities, relaxing and enjoying the island.

Sunday is always a quiet day on the island, and our first Sunday was no different than usual. Mike and I spent some time at the pool. We also rode around the island to see what had changed and what was still the same. We didn't go into Philipsburg, the capital of the Dutch side of the island, or into Marigot, the capital of the French side. It was just a very relaxing day.

We went to Orient Bay for lunch. Orient Bay is one of the prettiest of the thirty-seven beaches on the island. There is a restaurant there, Kakao, that has pizza that we love. We always like to sit right on the beach and enjoy a great view of the ocean and the water sports like wind surfing, parasailing, and boating. It's relaxing and entertaining just to sit on the beach at the restaurant and watch everything going on. Things appeared normal to us on this Sunday.

We returned to our resort by midafternoon because Addy Richardson, one of our favorite island musicians, was scheduled to sing at Tortuga, the restaurant at our resort.

Addy played island music and sang for three hours. He was as glad to see us as we were to see him. Mike and I and a few others danced the afternoon away.

Later, we went to Moomba, the bar next to our resort. We chatted with the young waiter, who was from Holland, and with his girlfriend, who arrived shortly after we did. Both of them were talking about the hurricane, expressing hope that St. Maarten would be spared from the storm.

Monday arrived, and Mike and I went to Philipsburg for our first stop, as always, to see our friends at Joe's Jewelry on Front Street. It was by happenstance that we met our now friends at Joe's Jewelry, and especially our favorite jeweler, Ron, one of our early years on the island.

We reconnected with Ron, Harry, and all of the Joe's Jewelry staff. Many of them have been at the shop most of the years we have been coming. We have grown a lovely history with our friends there over these seventeen years. Our oldest daughter's engagement and wedding rings were purchased at Joe's in 2001. In 2016, when we arrived on St. Maarten, we were welcomed by a beautiful flower arrangement in our suite from Joe's. It was an unexpected and delightful surprise.

Our friends at the shop know about the work and speaking I do. We had talked about the personality profiling questionnaire I developed years ago to use in my consulting work. Harry wanted to profile all of the staff, so we did that in 2016. We even profiled the owners of Joe's! I debriefed everyone so they would understand their data and how to use the information so they could better understand their own behavior and how to work well with each other and with customers. It was great fun seeing them get excited about what they learned about themselves and each other. Most of the staff are of Indian descent, so it was especially interesting to me when they validated the accuracy of their data just as others, usually U.S. Americans, have.

I had brought questionnaires with me, thinking Harry might want to do some reprofiles and profile anyone who was new to the team. We never got to that because they had become consumed with discussing Hurricane Irma. Harry was following the European model, and he was convinced that St. Maarten would suffer a direct hit.

While I was in the shop, a necklace with a beautiful square sapphire caught my eye. I bought it, and I am so glad I did, because I wear that necklace quite often now, and without fail, I receive compliments on it. This makes me happy because it is a constant reminder of our friends on St. Maarten.

The particular date of August 28, which falls during our annual get-away, brings to mind several memories for me. For one thing, it is the anniversary of my first marriage. Although the marriage did not last, it gave me a great gift—my daughter Tara, the daughter who became engaged on St. Maarten in 2001 and whose rings were purchased from Ron at Joe's Jewelry.

August 28 is also close to another anniversary. It is the

day before Hurricane Katrina hit and devasted New Orleans in the wee hours of the morning of August 29, 2005. New Orleans has always been another special place for Mike and me. Visiting New Orleans in the aftermath of Katrina and seeing the devastation the storm left behind was the stimulus for my year of no spending and the book from that experience, *A Year in the Life of a Recovering Spendaholic*. The loss of life and property that resulted from Katrina made me want—need—to take a new view of personal possessions. I succeeded in my year of no personal spending, but it took me ten years to finish preparing the book.

As the week continued on St. Maarten, I spent time at the pool. I glanced at the books in the lending library and saw the book *Hamilton*. A book club I belong to was reading *Hamilton*, and I had not yet purchased it, so I decided to check it out and begin reading it on this trip. That book became a constant companion during my remaining days on St. Maarten.

The next time Mike and I visited with Ron at the shop, he invited us to come to his home and participate in their prayer service on Saturday night. He said there would be a few others in addition to his wife, Muskaan, eleven-year-old son Sameer, and seventeen-month-old son Veer, and us. Although we did not know anything about a Muslim prayer service, we were honored to be invited and accepted his invitation to attend.

Life continued quite normally as the week progressed. Every year as we explore the St. Martin side of the island, we find changes, especially in Marigot. We made our usual tour. Although the French side of the island is less commercialized than the Dutch side, every Wednesday and Saturday, there is a wonderful outdoor market. You can always find the usual tourist items including hats, bags, small kitchen items, and many other things that are fun gifts to take home. There also are a few vendors who have lovely, authentic goods made in France such as table linens. I do love entertaining and hosting special meals, so I have enjoyed buying beautiful cotton tablecloths and napkins through the years, both for our home and for gifts.

There is also a spice man who has spices in bulk as well as spices packaged in small gift baskets. He is quite popular with the locals as well as with the tourists. Then there is the man who has fruit flavored rum that can be sampled to find your special flavor. We and a number of family and friends have become Banana Vanilla fans! The market restaurants offer superb creole and Caribbean food.

There is a different ambience on the French side of the island compared to the Dutch side. On the French side, most of the shopkeepers are of French nationality, and French remains their primary language. Most of the merchants understand English enough to communicate with the customers. The shop hours are abbreviated, and many shops close for two to three hours midafternoon. Some shops and restaurants close for the whole of the month of September and don't reopen until early or mid-October, the busy season for the island.

The Dutch side feels more "Americanized," which is

expressed by most people speaking English and the somewhat faster pace of life than the French side. Typically, the shops are open all day. Some do close during the slower September season, but not as many as St. Martin. It is interesting that on the Dutch side, many of the store staff are from India. Mike and I don't mind the few seasonally closed shops and restaurants during our vacation time on the island. After all, there is also less traffic, and we like that!

Mike and I always travel around both sides of the island, so we explored the Dutch side as well. Our annual island tour is partly from curiosity about what has happened while we have been gone, but I have to say change of all kinds interests me—what changes occur, why they happen, and how they are accommodated—what adjustments are made. I have noticed some changes in the Marigot market as well as economic changes in general on both sides of the island over the years.

In the earlier years of our travel to the island, the shopping was more robust with more expensive items available. Over the past decade that changed. I cannot know for sure, but the financial crisis the U.S. suffered, which was most dramatic in 2008 and 2009, may be a major factor for some of these changes. Many of the visitors to St. Maarten/St. Martin have been and still are from the U.S., and what affected the U.S. economy and spending power may well have had a direct effect on the economy of this Caribbean island. Higher end and luxury items are not so readily available in shops, and some of the shops that carried these products have even closed. Change of the hardest kind.

The weather in late August and early September in the Caribbean is usually predictable; it's hot and humid. When friends comment on this, my response is, "It is hot and humid in North Carolina at this time of the year too!" It's also hurricane season in both areas at this time of the year.

I admit my perspective on the weather issue has been reshaped. While hurricanes can and do occur in the U.S. as well as in the Caribbean in the months of August and September, the devastation suffered in places like the Caribbean is often more dramatic. The islands are not as well equipped to withstand or recover from devastation as we are in the U.S., although the U.S territories and areas within the continental U.S. have been sorely tested with catastrophic storms in the last two plus decades. I have to mention Hurricane Harvey. It hit several cities in Texas very hard landing on August 25, 2017, before impacting Louisiana and countries to our south—just a few days before Hurricane Irma landed on St. Maarten. Beaumont, Texas, a town to which I have an affinity, was one of the places Harvey ravaged. The *Beaumont Enterprise* has published several of my articles through the years. I seem to be connected to hurricanes or places where hurricanes hit, though I am not sure why.

The next time we went back to Joe's, Ron talked about moving his family into the Holland House Hotel on Front Street in Philipsburg, believing they would be safer there than in their apartment. He was not sure the apartment would be able to weather the effects of the wind and rain. Mike invited Ron and his family to move in with us and Harry too. Harry thought his home would be safe, but Ron decided to think about coming to stay with us.

At this point, Mike and I had not even talked about evacuating from St. Maarten. I was becoming more unsettled about the impending weather as the days passed, but I must be honest and say that I did not want to miss a full week of our annual two-week vacation any more than Mike did. I just had a greater sense of discomfort about our situation. Once we did begin to talk about our options, I let Mike drive our decision about what to do about this. I am overall a very optimistic person, sometimes to the point of being naïve. I know that this does not take me off the hook and relieve me of any responsibility about our decision to stay or go.

Life was just going on with its usual routines on the island. Yes, preparations were being made and yes, Irma was a frequent conversation topic, but the days continued to look and feel otherwise normal. We went to the Greenhouse in Simpson Bay and sat on the beach. It was a peaceful and pleasant evening. The weather was beautiful. It was warm and breezy. As I recall, we had a delicious and beautiful sunset dinner, looking out at the still calm but beginning to be restless ocean. There were a few other tables filled, but not as many people out for dinner as was common. I do not remember any talk of the hurricane that evening.

I was reading *Hamilton* Friday morning and finding to my surprise that I was actually enjoying a book about war.

The ocean was still beautiful. The weather had not yet begun to change, at least not to my hurricane novice eyes.

Saturday seemed to arrive quickly. Mike and I went into Philipsburg to discuss the evening worship service details with Ron. He suggested we come back and meet him at the store at five, and he would ride with us to his home.

Ron's home was small, and it sat high on a hill. As is the case with many homes in the area, there was no air conditioning. There were only two rooms in the apartment, the front room which included a small kitchen area and then the bedroom. The bedroom mainly included a very large bed, larger than a king bed. All four of the family slept in that bed. The front room, like the bedroom, was sparsely furnished. It had a long sofa and not much else. The feeling of love and welcome in the home overcame any thoughts about what "stuff" might be missing. It was obviously the home of people who were close emotionally as well as physically. This was very clear in how Ron and Muskaan interacted with each other and with the children.

Muskaan was preparing food for the evening when we arrived. We hadn't been there long when a few more people joined us. Muskaan offered food to everyone. I have forgotten the names of the food, although one was a soup.

Once the worship service began, Mike and I did our best to follow the lead of the others. We stood together in a circle, and prayer, which was more like chanting, was voiced by all. The fragrance of incense filled the room.

Ron and Muskaan were very gracious, helping us at different times to understand how to participate, yet never making us feel awkward. We felt very honored to be invited to this holy service, to feel as one with our friends and their friends of a different religion than ours. Different, but in some ways the same. Prayer. Holding hands. Singing. The feeling of honoring each other and our God was strong.

Thinking back on this experience, I do not recall any discussion about the impending weather conditions. I do not think this service had anything to do with weather.

Sunday we went to the Sunset Bar and Grill for lunch. It is an oddly famous place where people on the nearby beach can watch arriving airplanes being buffeted by Caribbean winds that blow even on normal weather days. There are clear warnings posted to stay off the beach when the planes are coming in, but many people do not heed the warnings. Just a few days earlier, a woman was killed when she was blown into the airport fence by the turbulence of a plane landing. It was both sad and alarming. That was the first time I had heard of an accident like that. Even with all of the warnings, the danger didn't seem quite real until hearing about this sad event. After that I had a different awareness and yet another change in perspective. Pay attention to warnings…

By now, the hurricane warnings were getting stronger, but the planes were still flying in. This was a bit surprising to me then and now when I think back on that time. Earlier, I had reconnected with a woman and her daughters whom I had met several years before when the girls were very young. I was shocked to see that they had grown up! They had just arrived on St. Maarten that day. I asked her about coming to the island when Hurricane Irma was expected to land in a couple of days. She said they discussed not coming but decided to come anyway. For a few moments in that conversation, I can remember thinking that if the planes were still flying in, and if people were still coming, things would probably be okay. That did not prove to be true.

Calvin and Erica and the other Tortuga staff were getting increasingly more worried. There was no musician today. All of the conversation was about Hurricane Irma. The latest prediction was that the storm would arrive on St. Maarten as a category 4, possibly a 5, on Tuesday or Wednesday.

By now, the resort staff had posted signs instructing everyone to prepare for the worst and that water and food should be secured.

Still, Mike and I did nothing to try to leave St. Maarten. To this day, I am shocked about that. I believe I was in denial. I have no idea where Mike's mind was. For some reason (maybe that denial) and despite all the warnings, I was not yet overly concerned. I was ignoring signs and discontinuities from our usual vacation experience.

On Monday, we made another visit into Philipsburg and stopped by Joe's. Ron and Harry were convinced that Hurricane Irma would make a direct hit on St. Maarten and were making plans. Ron told us that he would take us up on our offer to move his family in with us. We planned that they would come to our resort the next day.

Mike and I stayed in Philipsburg for lunch at Taloula Mango's. It wasn't very crowded. It was obvious from the streets, stores, and restaurants that people were heeding the warnings and apparently were either elsewhere preparing for the hurricane or had left the island. But not us. We had done neither.

In the early afternoon, Mike and I went back to our condo. I had begun asking Mike, at times I confess, heatedly, to look into options to get us off St. Maarten. I no longer wanted to assume that things would be fine. How could so many people be wrong? I most assuredly did not want to meet Hurricane Irma and was by then more concerned about our safety than I was about merely losing a week of our vacation time.

Mike checked the Internet, and the news was not good. American Airlines had no seats on the few planes that were going out of St. Maarten to any location. Since we had return tickets for the following week with them, American was our best option. The problem was there were no seats available on any flight on any carrier to any U.S. location.

Then an option opened up. We could take a flight from St. Maarten to Puerto Rico before Hurricane Irma was due to arrive. Mike booked tickets on that flight but continued to search for other options. We began watching the weather forecasts. There was more troubling news. In addition to Hurricane Irma, Hurricane Jose was headed to St. Maarten. And both were expected to hit Puerto Rico after leaving St. Maarten.

Mike and I discussed what to do. Given all of the variables, we decided that our best option was to stay on St. Maarten. We knew we had shelter and food here. We did not know what we would find in Puerto Rico. Mike cancelled our flight to Puerto Rico.

After our decision was made, we knew we needed to get supplies. We went to a grocery store across from our resort and to a sandwich shop. We were preparing to be without power. My concern about what we could face continued to rise.

Our family back home had been urging us for several days to leave St. Maarten, worried about our safety. As I have already said, I don't know why I was not more concerned earlier, but that was rapidly changing. I cannot speak for Mike, but to me, he did not seem unduly concerned about our situation—a little concerned but taking things in stride.

That said, we still were emotionally and physically exhausted, or at least I was, so we went to bed early. There was only one more day before we would meet Irma.

By Tuesday, the resort staff had already boarded up our condo with hurricane shutters on all of the sliding glass doors and moved all of the deck furniture inside. We had chosen "our" condo at the resort because of all the beautiful windows facing the ocean. It was depressing and distressing to see them securely boarded now. We could not see what was happening outside unless we went outside. I was unable to stay inside.

This is our Royal Islander resort, a few hours before Hurricane Irma arrived.

We knew Ron and his family were arriving at our resort around two, so Mike and I went to lunch a little early to make sure we were back in time. Of course, the conversation at the restaurant was all about Irma and Jose. By now it was clear to everyone that Irma was coming to St. Maarten, and she was expected to be devastating. It was not as clear what Jose would do. One man we spoke with had just arrived to St. Maarten with his boat two days before. Poor timing, indeed. This was our next to last meal before Irma.

When we arrived back at our resort a little before two, Ron and his family were there. They decided to keep their family together in one bedroom as was their custom. The bedroom they chose was next to ours and was the only bedroom with unboarded windows since this room was on the road side of the resort, whereas the other bedrooms were on the beach side.

Sameer goes swimming.

Once they were settled in, I decided to take Sameer to the pool. The weather was warm and breezy and obviously starting to change. We stayed at the pool and did not venture out on the beach, but I could see the ocean from where we were. The winds were causing the ocean water to "pick up." I knew this was likely to be the last few hours of calm that any of us would see for a while. We spent about an hour in the pool and talked with several other guests who were taking the same opportunity.

One of the people I talked with was a woman who worked for the U.S. State Department. She mentioned to me that she had been on the phone all day working to get as many U.S. citizens as possible off St. Maarten and back to the U.S. before the storm arrived. While the details were not all worked out yet, she was hopeful that she would be successful. (Several days later, after Irma had come and gone and Jose had moved out to sea, she walked a group of people from our resort to board U.S. military planes to Puerto Rico.)

After our pool time, Sameer and I went back inside and played games for a while. When dinnertime came, Mike and I decided we wanted to go out for what would probably be our last prepared meal for who knew how long. Ron and Muskaan had brought food supplies with them and decided to stay in with the children.

Not wanting to venture out too far, Mike and I walked next door to Moomba. One would think I would remember what we ate for our "last meal," but I don't. I was in a fog. I was trying hard not to let fear consume me. Fear is a dangerous emotion. When we are consumed by fear, we are not able to think clearly. I did not know what actions and decisions Mike and I would need to make over the next few days and being consumed by fear would adversely affect our ability to make the best decisions. We would need to be able to deal with whatever changes came our way. We would need to remain confident and clear-headed.

While I was finishing the writing of this book, I saw a segment on the *Megan Kelly Today Show* about fear. Michelle Poler, a young woman who had many fears, made the decision to do one thing a day that she was afraid to do for 100 days. Poler said she embarked on the 100 Fears in 100 Days project to become a braver person. Her number one fear was speaking in public. Now she has a TED talk about her experiences and is speaking publicly and confidently around the world about conquering fear.

Another person on the *Megan Kelly Today Show*, Kristen Ulmer, a former professional extreme skier, wrote a book titled *The Art of Fear*. She said being brave is not about being fearless. Ulmer said that there is no such thing as being fearless; it is about being brave. She also said there is unproductive fear and productive fear and that productive fear propels us to action while unproductive fear immobilizes us. During our Hurricane Irma experience, there was no time for unproductive fear. We had decisions to make. We had other people to think about, not just ourselves.

We went back to the condo and spent some time talking with Ron and Muskaan and playing games with Sameer. We all went to bed, knowing it would be a difficult night and probably an early morning. Irma was only a few hours away.

PART II

The Storm

Eye of the Storm

"Don't worry about the car; just stay safe." This was from a representative of the car rental agency on St. Maarten from whom we had rented our car for our two-week stay. Mike and I had gone to the office the day before Hurricane Irma was due to arrive to arrange returning our rental car to their care. The rental car agency representative was concerned about our safety, not the car, and encouraged us to keep it. As it turned out later, the rental car agency and its cars on the lot were mostly demolished. Our rental car had been parked underground and sustained no damage at all.

Mike and I had gone to bed around nine o'clock, knowing Irma would arrive in the early morning. I was not sleepy, so I read for a while. Our daughter Tara called at 9:21 p.m. and left a message that went to voicemail. I still have that message and will keep it forever. Her message was, "I don't know why this won't go through, but you'll stay safe, and we love you." I was able to call her back and reach her, and she comforted me. Her words, "You're going to be fine, Mom. You are going to be terribly inconvenienced for a few days, but you will be fine…" made me feel calmer. The promise in those words stayed with me throughout the next few days, and I replayed them in my mind when I needed them the most. With those words of comfort, our roles reversed. For most of her life I had been her comforter, now she was mine.

At 5:45 a.m. on Wednesday, September 6, 2017, I was awakened by howling winds and rain. It was obvious Irma had arrived. I got up and went into the bathroom. I took my computer and started writing. Hurricane Irma was at that very moment passing over St. Maarten. Mike stayed in bed for another hour, then he joined me in the bathroom—a safer room where there was no outside window or wall. Ron and his family were safe in the bedroom next to ours. We had done what we could to prepare for the worst and still hope for the best.

I worked on myself to stay calm. I was helped by texts, emails, and Facebook postings of love and prayers from many family members and friends stateside. I kept pictures of our granddaughters in front of me, praying for the gift of life to see them again. (Our grandson was not yet born.) The winds raged outside at greater than 185 miles an hour, a cruel reminder of nature's power and wrath.

While I was more frightened than I have ever been, I was also grateful. I was grateful for a strong building that was protecting us from the ravages of this storm. I was grateful for all the local people who spent days preparing for this impending devastation, knowing they would be left behind to pick up the pieces long after we tourists had returned home. Later, I was grateful for generators that kicked in soon after the power went off. I was grateful for food and water that we had that would sustain us for the days when we couldn't get out. I was grateful for our friends who were with us. Having a seventeen-month-old baby and an eleven-year-old boy and their parents going through this with us kept my fear in perspective. I was grateful for the resort staff who endangered themselves by going room-to-room to make sure their guests were safe.

In the days after, I had much more to be grateful for. This experience was such a testament to the reality that during our storms, literal and otherwise, there is always something to be grateful for. Keeping thoughts of gratitude in focus helped calm my fear, as did writing about the experience while I was living it.

When the eye of Irma passed over us, it gave us about an hour of calm. During that time, we put towels and bedspreads down to manage some of the water that had come in. We had lost a skylight window and that provided an open portal for the rain. After the eye passed, the winds and rain started up again as Irma continued its path over St. Maarten. By then, all six of us were huddled in our bathroom, the place we felt would be the safest in the storm. I even brought two water noodles we had to the

Our friends Ron (whose true name is Arun), Sameer, Muskaan, and Veer weathered the storm with us.

bathroom in case the water came in and we had to swim!

I was and still am grateful for the prayers that many prayed for us during the storm and continued to pray for our safety and well-being after the storm. As hard as it was to be in the middle of this fierce wind and rain, I imagine it was harder for our family not knowing how we were faring. I prayed, not just for us in the storm and our safety, but also for our loved ones, for peace that passes all understanding.

About seven hours after the hurricane landed, it was gone, headed elsewhere, eventually making its way to Florida and Georgia. We were left in our condo with water everywhere and power from a generator. There was no air conditioning or running water, and the hurricane shutters remained on the windows for the rest of our stay due to Hurricane Jose's expected arrival. We remained in our unit with those conditions until we were evacuated four days later. Thankfully, St. Maarten and we were spared a second hurricane. Hurricane Jose did not arrive.

Hurricane Irma and St. Maarten

During the night of September 6, we knew we had survived the storm. Mike and Ron decided to venture out despite the mandatory 24-hour curfew. The military had not yet arrived, and it was possible to be out without being stopped by roadblocks. However, so many cars were on the road that the drive took much longer than normal. In fact, there was nothing normal about anything at that point.

Sonesta, the hotel next to our resort, was so damaged that all guests had to be evacuated.

Mike and Ron drove what is normally a thirty-minute drive to Ron's home to see what damage his family's apartment had suffered.

They returned five hours later reporting some of the roads were almost impassable. They had found what they expected at Ron's home. The roof was gone, and most of the family's belongings were destroyed. They gathered what food was salvageable and a few other items and brought them back to the condo.

The next day all six of us ventured out to go to Ron's home again to get more of their family's belongings and to determine the condition of the main shopping area of Philipsburg where the jewelry store is located. By this time the military had arrived and set up roadblocks, so it was slow going to get anywhere. Looters were all over the streets, carrying large TVs and other electronics they had stolen, and the police were apparently unable to stop them. Looters also wiped out the grocery stores so there was no food left in them.

Front Street in downtown Philipsburg after the storm

The road to Ron's home was now closed to traffic from the part of the island where we were. The main shopping area had suffered significant damage, both from Irma and from looters. What the storm had not damaged, looters had. They had damaged or removed hurricane shutters on the doors of the shops, broken the glass, and stolen whatever they could find within.

When we finally got to Joe's Jewelry, it was not possible to get in. It was in the same condition as the other businesses in the area. Ron said their jewelry had been well-secured in their preparations for the storm. He was hopeful whatever damage there was to the store would be reparable.

From Wednesday, September 6 until Sunday, September 10, Mike and I continued to try to evacuate from St. Maarten. Princess Juliana airport had suffered significant damage, and there were no commercial planes flying in or out. Military planes did come in, delivering welcome supplies. Eventually those same military planes took Americans out, although there was no organized plan for doing so and no communication about transport other than word of mouth. It was difficult to know what to believe. From what we heard, the people who left by military plane did so by walking to the airport and waiting in long lines for many hours. It was also reported that those successful in getting out by a military plane would only be able to take one piece of luggage, and it would have to rest in the passenger's lap during the flight.

We did know that the military planes were taking the Americans to San Juan. Once there, the passengers would be responsible for getting their own local lodging and arranging their own flight home. By the time we heard of this option, we were concerned about the number of people who had vacated to San Juan already and the potential for being unable to find a hotel room or a flight home. We talked about our options and decided we were safer staying where we were on St. Maarten.

During those days after the storm, there was no communication on the island other than word of mouth; no phone service, no Internet, no cable, and no radio for most of those days. We had food, although it would not last more than a few days. And we were fortunate to have power because of generators. We never did regain running water, although some units in our resort did have water.

We spent our time just sitting and talking. The time passed slowly. I did read some, as I recall, but I could not seem to concentrate on or find interest in my book. I did not have any energy to write, though with the time on my hands, I could have written a book! I think I was in a state of shock and did not want to do anything but wait to go home.

Mike, Sameer, Patti, Muskaan, Veer, and Ron saying goodbye

There was no organized evacuation plan for several days. Not surprisingly, the locals wanted and needed the tourists to go home. Caring for and keeping safe the 6,000 tourists during such extreme circumstances strained all their limited resources. While our unit suffered minimal storm damage, other units in our resort were damaged beyond usage. People in other resorts told of being placed in large conference rooms, sleeping on cots, and being without toilet facilities readily available. The stories from others made us once again realize how very fortunate we were compared to many. Our resort staff did unbelievable and admirable work through all this, leaving their own damaged or destroyed homes to come to work to care for their guests.

A prime concern for the resort staff was the matter of tourist safety. The looting in the streets had turned to violence in the resorts. Men with machetes were overtaking security guards and robbing tourists. The resort staff at our property asked us to remain in our rooms and not risk the violence that was all around us. We occasionally left our unit to visit others in our resort and to get food from the restaurant across the street that cooked and sold meals a couple of those days. We also needed to find out what others knew about the possibility of getting off the island.

Saturday night about eleven, three nights after Hurricane Irma's passage, a resort representative came to our unit with an evacuation plan. We were told to be in the lobby at seven a.m. the next day with all our luggage. She said a bus would pick us up and take us to Philipsburg to be evacuated by a cruise ship. There were no other details provided. We would leave our friends behind, and they would need to leave our resort when we did. Ron and his family had an offer of lodging from a local friend, and their plan was to move in with that family until they could decide what to do next.

Our Evacuation Options

Mike and I were in the lobby Sunday *before* seven a.m. Ron and his family left the resort when we went to the lobby. It was a tearful goodbye. We worried about what would happen to them, when/if we would see them again, and when we would see our beautiful island alive and vibrant once more. Eight hours later, we were still waiting for the bus to take us to the cruise ship.

There were about thirty of us waiting to leave. During our long wait in the lobby, we stood a lot, sat some, talked, and even ate breakfast the resort staff provided us. The respite provided by the breakfast nourished us as much as the food did. We all were in an "on hold" mindset, waiting. There was little information provided by anyone during this time.

A little before noon, a Royal Caribbean cruise ship was spotted passing by our resort. There was an immediate outbreak of applause and cheers. Seeing a cruise ship was welcome confirmation that we actually were going to be evacuated. This was the first that I knew which cruise ship was going to rescue us. It was Royal Caribbean's *Adventure of the Seas*.

During the more than eight hours that we waited, there were several buses that came and went, but none to take us to the cruise ship. There was a truck loaded with our luggage parked nearby. We waited and waited.

Some asked questions about when the bus was coming ("soon"), why it hadn't arrived yet ("it had taken some people to the airport and would be back soon"), and what time the cruise ship was to sail ("five p.m."). When three p.m. came and went and still no bus, the unrest in the group was palpable. We all knew the drive across the island to the cruise ship terminal could take us a long time given the road conditions, and we began to fear the cruise ship would leave without us. Hope began to turn to hopelessness. We thought what had seemed too good to be true, being rescued soon, might actually be just that—too good to be true.

In addition to the cruise ship evacuation option, there still were those military plane evacuations. No mention was made by anyone, to my knowledge, about any cost involved with either option. I did wonder about the cost but did not want to make any decision based on that, so I did not verbalize the question, not even to Mike. I remember thinking that if there was a cost, that whatever the cost was, it would be worth it. I also remember thinking that if there was a cost that we likely would have been told, since "they" would need to be sure that we were prepared to pay it.

There were some in our resort who did elect to take the military plane option developed by the woman I met at the pool who worked with the U.S. State Department. There was much discussion back and forth among those waiting about which evacuation option they elected and why. Those who elected the military plane option left in the morning and walked the two miles to the airport, each taking with them the one lap-size suitcase they were allowed to take. Those of us who remained at the resort received no information about how they fared.

When Mike and I had discussed the alternatives and

decided to take the cruise ship, our decision included the difficulty posed by the military plane option. We did not relish repacking our belongings into one suitcase each, having to walk two miles to the airport carrying the bags, and then holding the bags on our laps during the flight. It wasn't about leaving behind our "stuff" as much as it was the sheer energy required to elect this option. We were told we could be waiting in line for hours outside of the airport in the heat.

People at our resort waited in line for many hours to be evacuated.

All this and the concern we had had earlier about being able to get a hotel room in San Juan and a flight back to the U.S. when there were already so many people trying to do the same thing tipped the scale for our decision to wait for the cruise ship. And not for one minute did I think this would be a cruise that would be enjoyable; it would be an evacuation ship.

When hours passed, and hope was almost gone, our bus finally arrived! We boarded the bus quickly and were on our way. Once the bus started moving, my fear again turned to hope. I think all of us on the bus finally allowed ourselves to believe that we were going to be evacuated and that we would be on our way home soon. I was surprised that the drive to the cruise ship did not take as long as we all had feared it would.

Our evacuation ship, Royal Caribbean's Adventure of the Seas, *came to St. Maarten to take 300 Americans to safety.*

Soon Royal Caribbean's *Adventure of the Seas* was visible. We were almost there—the place to disembark from the bus with the next step to be boarding the ship that would deliver us home or rather nearer to home. We were close to beginning our circuitous route back to the U.S.

But not so fast. The guards who came to the bus driver's window said the ship was full. There was no room for us. We were told to turn around and go back. The bus driver said he was out of gas; he could not make it back. Now, not only did it seem that the ship would not accept us, but what were we to do? The resort had released us and might not allow us to come back, if we could even *get* back.

This was my second lowest point of the entire Hurricane Irma experience. (My lowest point had been when the hurricane was passing over us, and I truly believed that I was going to die by being ripped from our resort and thrown into the Atlantic Ocean or against our concrete building.) The fear I felt with this news was all about the absolute unknown of what we would do now that our Royal Caribbean life boat had sunk. To be so close to being evacuated from the devastation of Hurricane Irma on St. Maarten, to be at the cruise ship gate, only to be turned away was demoralizing to say the least. I think on some subconscious level, I was more worried about what could happen to us *before* we might die. My mind swirled with these thoughts and fears.

An Adventure of the Seas

WAIT! Our bus driver was in solution mode. He was not to be deterred by guards and gates. He called the person who had confirmed that we were to be on the ship. She told him what to do, who the contact was from the ship, and instructed him to tell the ship's representative that we were confirmed to be on the ship, that we were included in their number. When the ship representative came to the bus and waved us in, there were shouts of joy from all on our bus! I can't remember another time that I had felt such despair and such joy in the same few minutes.

We disembarked from the bus, went through security, collected our bags, and then were led to the cruise ship to board. The walk from the bus to the cruise ship was surreal. That was the first time that I allowed myself fully to believe that we were *really* being evacuated. It was finally feeling real.

There was still little information available to us. The only thing that we were told was that once we boarded the ship we were to go to the ship's conference room. In the conference room, the first things I saw were snacks and soft drinks. That was the beginning of Royal Caribbean feeding us literally and figuratively. We were given an information sheet with instructions on how to connect to the Internet. They even provided complimentary Internet access for us for the length of our shipboard stay. That was the first time in days we were able to connect by email or to connect at all.

According to the information sheet, Royal Caribbean was providing us with free laundry and dry-cleaning services for the length of our stay. How did they know that these two things—to be connected to our families and friends and to have clean clothes—would meet our most important needs at that moment? To have come from the damage and destruction we had left to now being on a beautiful cruise ship cared for in such a manner was almost beyond belief to me.

There was still no mention of any cost that we would incur for this evacuation. We were checked in, given our room assignments, and taken through a safety demonstration. Then we were able to go to our assigned staterooms.

Royal Caribbean's *Adventure of the Seas* is a large cruise ship. This ship of three thousand guests and one thousand crew members was on a scheduled cruise that rerouted to St. Maarten to pick up three hundred Americans to take us to safety. This was clearly a humanitarian effort.

We were soon told that our passage was complimentary. Our room and board, Internet, and laundry—everything was complimentary. A phone was even made available for us to use to call home, book flights, or for whatever we needed. All of this was provided for us by Royal Caribbean. Contrast this with those who evacuated by military plane. We were told later that they had to sign a promissory note to repay the U.S. government the cost of a one-way plane ticket from St. Maarten to San Juan.

The *Adventure of the Seas* cruise originated in San Juan and came to St. Maarten on Sunday, September 10. From St. Maarten, the ship was going to Curacao, then to Aruba, Bonaire, and back to San Juan on Saturday, September 16. Those of us being evacuated were encouraged to take the entire cruise at no cost, although we were able to evacuate at any port from which we could get a flight home. The accommodations were lovely, the food was delicious, and the service was thoughtful and excellent. Royal Caribbean could not have been more gracious and generous with us. But I still wanted to be home.

Our daughter Tara had been in frequent contact with American Airlines trying to get us home. Now that we had Internet access, Mike was trying as well. The problem was most flights from the cruise ship ports went through Miami, and the Miami airport was still closed due to the hurricane there. Our best option was to fly from Aruba to Charlotte, North Carolina, and then to Raleigh so that was what we planned to do.

We shared a meal with our resort friends with whom we are now bonded forever.

It seemed to me that those of us who had evacuated from the Royal Islander, our St. Maarten resort, were now in a special club. There were about ten couples/families in this "club." From that point on, we would be going in different directions with most taking the cruise ship all the way to San Juan. While we might not ever see each other again after we reached the U.S., for this point in time, we were bonded. I decided to ask all of those I could find to meet for dinner on Monday night. We had a wonderful time of connecting and sharing before our next port of call.

The first port was Curacao. While Mike and I did go ashore there, we stayed close to the ship and returned aboard before long. The next port was Aruba, and we arrived on Wednesday morning, September 13. When we left the ship late afternoon in Aruba, I had conflicting emotions. I was glad to be getting closer to home, yet aware that I was leaving behind people with whom we had shared a unique experience. These were not family nor even friends in the traditional sense; we only had this shared experience. But now we would be a part of each other's history forever. Along with the excitement about being closer to home, there was sadness about leaving behind these people.

I was also aware that we were now on our own. For the past few days, we had been cared for by Royal Caribbean. They fed us, made our beds, washed our clothes, and made sure we had connection with the outside world. All of that would now be up to us. I was not so sure we were ready for that.

Our peaceful oasis at the Aruba Hilton

Mike had booked a room for us as we were scheduled to fly home the next day. After having a quiet meal and a good night's sleep, we headed to the airport in plenty of time to catch our afternoon flight.

Our American Airlines flight boarded around four p.m. on Thursday, September 14. After the usual pre-boarding and boarding details, our plane was ready to take off. We began to taxi down the runway. But instead of ascending into the air, our plane came to a screeching halt. I remember wondering if we had hit another plane, although it did not feel like a collision, or if maybe we had had a flat tire. I have flown many times and have never had such an abrupt stop. It was not clear what was happening.

After a few minutes that seemed much longer, the pilot

came on the intercom and told us to stay seated because we were returning to the gate.

My heart sank.

The Saga Continues

Just when we thought we were headed home, we turned back to the gate instead. A mechanical problem was the culprit. Over the intercom, the pilot reported that diagnosing and correcting the problem would probably take a couple of hours. We were instructed to deplane and wait near the gate. There really wasn't anywhere else to wait. The lounge near the gate was now closed, as was everything else. At times we paced, unable to sit still. We talked to other passengers and heard some interesting stories.

One man who was headed to Charlotte had been in Aruba for more than a week attending a convention. He was scheduled to leave Aruba the previous Sunday. His flight had been cancelled, and he and his sister, who was with him, had not been able to get on another flight home until that day; all the other flights were full. He said they were fine, that their additional expenses for lodging and food were covered by his company, but that some were not so fortunate. He told of a family with a child who had been staying at an all-inclusive resort, travelling on a shoestring. When their flight was cancelled, they had to relocate to another hotel, barely able to afford that and the food they needed for the five additional days.

About an hour after we deplaned, we were told that another flight was due in from Charlotte soon and that the decision had been made to send us out on that plane. We learned that our original plane had been sitting at the airport for days, and the needed repair on it appeared to be more extensive than anticipated. We were relieved that there was another plane option. Or at least we thought there was.

The plane from Charlotte landed soon thereafter. Knowing that "turning around" a large plane takes about forty-five minutes, I became concerned when we were not boarding more than an hour later. By this time, making our connection from Charlotte to Raleigh was questionable. The longer we were in Aruba, the less likely it was that we would make that flight. Given that, Mike spoke to American Airlines through Skype and changed our connecting flight from Charlotte to Raleigh. Since our original flight from Charlotte was the last flight out that day, we would be spending the night in Charlotte. That was the plan anyway.

Another announcement was made. Not only would we not get out of Charlotte that night, it seemed that we would not even make it out of Aruba.

Unbelievable as it was, the plane that had arrived from Charlotte, the plane that was now supposed to take us to Charlotte, also had a mechanical problem! How likely is it that two planes in the same airport (Aruba), two planes from the same carrier (American), two planes headed to the same airport (Charlotte), would *both* have mechanical problems on the same day?

My mind went in several directions. Mike and I do travel frequently, so delays are not uncommon experiences for us. Typically, my thoughts go to being glad that they found the mechanical problem while the plane was on the ground even if the delay is inconvenient. This time, in Aruba, I knew this in my soul, but knowing it did not make that experience any easier. While my logical mind tried to deal with the delay, my emotional self was not able to be grateful in that moment. I was spent. I just wanted to go home.

I began to think of what we would do if we were stranded in Aruba. While we had resources, the family with the child that had been stranded earlier in the week apparently did not. What would happen for them? Where were they? And how were we to know that we could even get a hotel room at the last minute? And for how long would we need a hotel room? How would this latest delay affect our ability to get seats on another plane from Aruba to Charlotte? The flights from Aruba to Charlotte on subsequent days might all be full! I began to wish we were back on the cruise ship with our room and board secure with little to worry about other than how to avoid overeating.

But we weren't on the cruise ship. We were at the Aruba airport, and by then, we had been for almost seven hours.

Finally Going Home!

So, there we all were, waiting. Finally, an announcement was made that the mechanical problem had been resolved on the plane that had arrived earlier from Charlotte, and we were ready to board. Shouts of relief greeted that announcement as we made our way to the gate. The boarding process went quickly and smoothly. We were finally in the air about eight p.m., headed to Charlotte.

When we arrived in Charlotte around midnight, the American Airlines staff at the gate was ready for us. We were given vouchers for food and a hotel confirmation and were told that our bags would remain at the airport to be loaded for our flight the next morning. We picked up an amenity pack and boarded the hotel shuttle that carried us a few miles to a Days Inn. After about four hours of not so good sleep, we were back at Charlotte Douglas International Airport. I used the food vouchers for food that could travel with us, not at all interested in eating at that time. Our flight took off from Charlotte uneventfully and arrived in Raleigh on schedule.

A most welcome sight! Daughter Tara and granddaughters Mary Grace, Elsie, and Virginia welcome us home at the RDU Airport.

I have felt joy many times in my life, but none more heartfelt than the joy of seeing our daughter and granddaughters waiting for us as we came into the public area of the Raleigh Durham

Airport. Tara, Mary Grace, Elsie, and Virginia were holding "Welcome Home Nana and Dr. Danks!" signs. ("Dr. Danks" is their special name for Mike; the story about that another time). Daughter Chatham had picked up our luggage. She and Mike drove to our home together, while I rode home with Tara and the girls. Home was such a welcome relief. We were greeted there by many other "Welcome Home" signs as well as balloons, fresh flowers, and a special treat for Dr. Danks. Mike loves pork rinds, and there was a bag of pork rinds on the kitchen counter for him!

There was much hugging and more than a few tears! Irma had devastated St. Maarten early in the morning on Wednesday, September 6. We had been evacuated from St. Maarten on Sunday afternoon, September 10. On Friday, September 15, we were back home in Raleigh with our family.

Our "Welcome Home" sign—that has become permanent—and flowers and pork skins!

Afterwards

In addition to feelings of joy, I had other emotions. Feelings of relief were dominant along with physical and emotional exhaustion. Little things took on significance. After the storm, there was no place for me to return my borrowed book due to the devastation of our resort so that copy of *Hamilton* now has a special place on my desk. It is quite worn from the wind and rain of the storm. I will keep this book and replace it with a new book for the lending library when we are able to return to our resort on the island.

Feelings of sadness came later. Then depression. Mike was not on the same emotional roller coaster as I. He rebounded from the Hurricane Irma experience quickly, seeing it more as an adventure than a crisis. I will not judge that or even analyze it. Mike left on a business trip to Taiwan less than twenty-four hours after we arrived back in Raleigh. I understood completely that he had to make the business trip and was glad that he was able to get home in time for it.

I spent the next few days enjoying being home, letting Tara and the girls, Chatham, and my very good friend MoMo cook and care for me that weekend. This is the only time that I remember being unable physically or emotionally to care for others. Just then, I needed to be cared for *by* others. I gave into that feeling and need and was glad that they were there to care for me.

Then Monday came, and with everyone's schedule, things had to get back to normal. Everyone's normal but mine. I had to find a new normal.

I had a case of PTSD, or at least a therapist friend of mine diagnosed that. She and others encouraged me to see a therapist. I chose not to do that, not because I do not believe in therapy, I do. I have had therapy and recommend it to others. But that was not what I wanted to do this time. I knew that I needed to heal, and I decided I could do so by looking within myself, talking with good friends, and self-nurturing.

My depression lasted for a couple of months. This was one of the few times I ever remember being depressed. I did not need a therapist, and I did not need medicine. I needed to find myself again, knowing it would not be the same self as before. An important person to my recovery was a life coach. Thank you, dearest Rivka. Although I did not have much energy and did not want to do much of anything, I made myself keep moving. Eventually, I found myself again, but it was not the same me.

When Hurricane Irma hit St. Maarten, it was the worst hurricane recorded anywhere, and that record still stands, even with the arrival of Hurricane Maria, the storm that struck San Juan, Puerto Rico, on September 20, 2017, destroying most of the city and doing massive damage to other islands. On September 19, 2017, a 7.1 magnitude earthquake decimated much of Mexico City. Now being safe at home, I was unable to write but needed to process what occurred with us and to others with all of the suffering around the world. I felt that I had to write before my experience and its lessons were too far removed from memory to teach the lessons I was to learn.

I am changed forever. Not just by Hurricane Irma. Hurricane Irma was the culmination of a series of events, none of which individually catapulted me into depression, but the combination of them did. No, that is not even right. Yes, 2017 was a very difficult year, and each of the car accidents and Irma contributed. But as I think back to the two years before, I had been awash in a career change, a change that had happened quickly, a change that I did not want and could not control. I had not dealt with all of that before the events of 2017 happened. In the meantime, I had lost myself, the self that I had been and had become comfortable with.

Looking back on this a year later, my feelings about staying on St. Maarten through the storm are mixed. I regret our family having fear about our safety and having to deal with that for days. I also will never forget my fear of dying and the fear and sense of loss of not being able to see our granddaughters grow into adults. I also believe that all things happen for a reason and that our greatest growth comes from conquering our greatest fears. That said, I have not yet reconciled my perspectives.

Still, when I thought I was going to die, I decided to really live. How that is manifesting in me is still evolving. Change happened and more changes will need to happen. And that's part of the story too.

Changes we do not want and cannot control do not have to result in depression or PTSD. In Part III of this book you will discover some tools that can help you deal with change, especially change that you do not want and cannot control. But before I get to the change lessons that have come from all this, there is one more part of the story to tell and that means another trip to St. Maarten.

St. Maarten One Year Later

On Saturday, September 1, 2018, Mike and I woke up early to get ready to head to the airport to board our flight to St. Maarten through Miami. While I was dressing, I heard the word "hurricane" on the TV and almost panicked. Mike knew I would, so he said, "It's in Japan." I had already checked on the weather earlier in the week and was assured that there were no hurricanes anywhere near St. Maarten and none were expected. I told our family that if there was any indication of any hurricane, I would not be going. Still, I think all of us (except Mike!) were nervous about this trip.

Walking to the gate at the Raleigh-Durham Airport, I was aware that my pace was quick and my energy level was high. I contrasted that to coming through this same airport from St. Maarten a year ago, feeling physically and emotionally exhausted. I certainly felt different preparing to fly to St Maarten this year than I had when we came home so exhausted last year, but I wondered what we would find once we got to St. Maarten. How much had the island recovered one year later?

My thoughts about the island's recovery made me reflect on what I had written already about my recovery journey from the 2017 events. How have I "recovered"?

- I do not think I will ever again take safety for granted. I am much more careful than I ever was before my 2017 events.

- I drive better now, am less distracted when driving, and drive more defensively. I hope that I will never again think of driving a vehicle as just getting from one place to another; a vehicle is also a moving object that can cause considerable harm to its occupants and to others. While that can happen when one is doing all things right, if it happens when one is distracted, the guilt from the damage to self and/or others is not worth whatever one was doing when the accident occurred. Driving is serious business.

- I prepare more than I did a year ago.

- Although I have recovered from most of the negative effects of the hurricane experience, this trip brings back some feelings of anxiety and even fear, especially a fear of the unknown.

- I am more vigilant about watching those around me, something I never thought of before much less worried about. Before Hurricane Irma, I had never seen looters and certainly not looters running down the street carrying large TVs and other electronics, never mind the looters with machetes we heard about! The memory of that is still strong a year later. Hopefully the negative memories of this experience will fade over time and only good memories and lessons learned will remain.

- I have learned the importance of paying attention, although sometimes I still fail to connect the signs with what they could mean. An example of this happened on our flight to St. Maarten. I got up to go to the restroom on the plane and was signaled back to my seat by the flight attendant. The pilots were out of the cockpit, and the entrance to the front was blocked. I had seen the table blocking the entry to the front where the restroom was but did not connect what that meant. A few minutes later when all was clear, the flight attendant apologized for my wait and explained this had been the rule since 9/11. I knew that but had never encountered it. I told her that I wasn't paying attention. She told me the following story.

> My daughter always has her face in her phone, and I had told her many times to get her face out of her phone and pay attention to what is going on around her, especially when on the subway! (She lives in New York City.) About six months ago, my daughter was attacked on the subway by someone who threw a chemical on her neck. She was rushed to the hospital and given an antidote for the chemical.

Her daughter recovered, thankfully. What a terrible way to learn the lesson of paying attention to what is going on around you! I hope this story shared with me will help all of us remember the important lesson of being observant.

As we were kept safe and cared for on our flight to St. Maarten, I was reminded of our rescue/evacuation ship after the hurricane. I will always remember how it felt to get on the ship and know we were safe, to have our first meal, which nourished us in more ways than nutritionally, and finally to be able to begin to relax. This American flight from Miami to St. Maarten, although not an evacuation flight, felt similar. This time instead of going home, we were going back to the storm area.

There was one difference I noticed from previous flights to St. Maarten and that was the absence of the *Destinations St. Maarten* magazine. In past years, each passenger was offered this magazine when boarding the plane, but not this time; no mention was made of it. Other than that, this flight felt no different than our eighteen plus previous flights to the friendly island of St. Maarten, although *I* felt different.

When our plane touched down on St. Maarten, the airport was not what I expected. When we first came to St. Maarten in 2000, the airport was almost third world. No air conditioning, gates that were subpar, and no modern conveniences. That had changed in the past few years. The airport had become very modern with all of the conveniences one would expect. This time, we were back to the airport of 2000. We arrived at a temporary building with limited air conditioning and no modern conveniences.

The main terminal was not open at all. Our arrival experience was not the usual one, and we could see people waiting in long lines to check in and surmised from that that our departure might be more difficult than our arrival. I was struck by this, wondering why a year later the airport had not been repaired to its pre-hurricane condition since tourism was the island's main economic engine. I later learned it was because of insurance delays. As the days passed and we toured the island several times, my perspective changed. My initial questions were answered.

Mike and I left the airport in the Thrifty Car Rental van, and soon thereafter were driving away in our rental car. When we left the airport, we saw boats wrecked by Hurricane Irma that had not been repaired or even moved. That was shocking and took me right back to the few days after the storm when we had ridden around and surveyed the damage and had seen these same boats.

This is one of the many wrecked boats still in the water.

When Mike and I were talking about our upcoming trip, I had told him that the first thing I wanted to do when we got to St. Maarten was to go to Joe's Jewelry. We don't usually go into Philipsburg the first day when we arrive on the island midafternoon. But this time, I had a strong need to see Ron, if only for a few minutes, to see that he was all right. I knew he was there, because we had emailed, but I wanted to see him and hear first-hand how he and his family were doing. Although I wanted to go to Joe's Jewelry and see Ron before doing anything else, we did stop by the hotel and register. It seemed odd not going to our usual resort.

Harry and Ron (L to R) of Joe's Jewelry; #1 on Trip Advisor

Thirty minutes after leaving the airport, we were at Joe's and happily greeting Ron, Harry, and some of the other staff. My heart was full! It seemed like any other year, not the first time back since our hurricane experience.

After leaving Joe's, Mike and I drove to the Maho area where the Royal Islander is located. As we expected, it was locked up, still under renovation. We then went to Sunset Beach Bar, next to our condo, where we could look at the ocean and see the progress on the Royal Islander. Then we drove back to the Atrium in the Simpson Bay area to get settled in our studio. A beautiful flower arrangement and a bottle of champagne from Ron and Joe's Jewelry greeted us. What a very special welcome back to our island! And our studio was lovely.

A surprise from Ron and from Joe's Jewelry was waiting for us!

Mike and I spent most of the day driving all over the island, all thirty-seven miles of it. It was our customary tour but with very different sights to see. The devastation all around was shocking. At first it was hard to believe that a year had passed and there was so much left to do. Destroyed homes and buildings, fallen or damaged trees, and foliage and other debris from the force of the wind and rain were so sad to see. Later as we saw more of the island, my perspective changed, and I was encouraged that so much repair and renovation had been done.

Simpson Bay, the area in which we were staying this year, was spared, for the most part, during Irma. Of all of the areas on both the Dutch and French side, Simpson Bay looked the best. Most of the resorts, restaurants, and shops appeared to be operating normally though one of Mike's favorite restaurants, Lee's Roadside Grill, was completely gone. We did hear that they closed up before the hurricane.

The Maho area on the Dutch side, where our property is located, was one of the hardest hit areas. We saw only two restaurants open in that area as well as the surprise of one new café. Most of the stores were still closed. While it was obvious that there was work going on, there still was much to be done. The two largest properties in Maho were both still closed. The Royal Islander plans to reopen in October of 2018, and the Sonesta Maho Beach Resort in February 2019.

Orient Beach, a popular area for beach restaurants and bars, only had one business open. The Bikini Beach Bar and Restaurant opened two months ago after being entirely rebuilt. Our favorite, Kakao, was gone completely, though we were told it is being rebuilt in another area of the beach. Mr. Busby's Beach Bar was also completely gone and not much was left of other places. The Westin resort was closed but slated to reopen. Some of the Oyster Pond area had been rebuilt, while other areas needed much repair.

We had heard that the French side of the island suffered the most damage, and we saw that as we toured. Many of the homes, resorts, and businesses on the French side will take some time to return to any semblance of normal. Many boats were still overturned in the water, something we saw on the Dutch side as well.

One good sign was that the locals were encouraged to see that tourism was returning. The cruise ships had started coming back to the island and with them came the island's major source of revenue. Nowadays, when the cruise ships are in port for one day, the cruise ship guests primarily see the main shopping areas unless they venture out and drive over the island. This means they do not see most of the devastation that has yet to be repaired.

The ocean and the beaches were still beautiful, although there was debris on some of the beaches. The water was as blue and clear as I remember it from our first visit.

On Monday, Mike and I started our day by riding to the Maho area to see who we could find at The Royal Islander. We were glad to find John, the Guest Relations Assistant Manager, and spent a few minutes talking with him. He said the Royal Islander still had a lot to be done to be ready to reopen as they planned in October.

Mike and John, the Royal Islander Guest Relations Assistant Manager, at the Royal Islander resort

Mike and I spent some time walking the Maho area to see the changes. We saw the new Cape Café. Interestingly enough, we had seen an advertisement for the business at Bikini Beach. We went in and sat down to talk to a young couple at the table next to us. She was from Brazil, he was from Russia, and they lived in Germany. I learned that they came to St. Maarten the first time four years ago, came back this past February, and are back this time for three weeks because they love the beaches.

As we talked, they commented on how many businesses were still in need of significant repair. I asked them their opinion about that, and the man said he thought it was because there were not enough workers to do the work. He said there needed to be more people able to get to St. Maarten who wanted to work, but because of the rigid work rules of the European Union, they couldn't get to the island. When I asked them how the conditions were now compared to when they were here in February, they both said the conditions were much better.

We also talked to the server, who is from the Netherlands. She said that the café opened in February and that it is owned by a man from Canada. It was very interesting to me that a new business would open in this area at this time. Perhaps this is a good example of entrepreneurship.

We went back to Joe's Jewelry to see our friends. Philipsburg was not as vibrant as I had hoped to find it; many of the shops were closed for renovation or perhaps for good. There were not many people in town, probably because there was no cruise ship in port. Still, several of the stores I recognized were open for business. We went to Taloula Mango's for lunch, then back to Ron's to consider some jewelry purchases. Ron said ours was the only purchase for the store that day.

The next day there was a cruise ship in port! That was good news for the island businesses. We visited Maho Beach to watch the people watching the planes come in. There was a large crowd. We also visited with a couple of staff at Royal Islander. We talked about the damage from Hurricane Irma, and one of them compared the clean-up from this hurricane to that from Hurricane Louis in 1995. She said that the clean-up from Hurricane Louis happened much quicker. She and others as well mentioned that people do not have the money to repair their properties this time.

We continued to visit other areas on the island. Some had very little damage, but in other areas, everything remained closed. The beach at Long Bay Beach, a beautiful beach in the exclusive area of Les Terres Basses, was totally deserted. The now closed luxury resort La Samanna is expected to reopen December 2018. We didn't hear anything about the state of the many mansions in the area behind concrete and stone walls. Like all of the 37 beaches on the island, this beach is a public beach, although one has to know that to be able to navigate to it.

Wednesday arrived—the anniversary of the day before Irma. Our first outing of the day was to the Marigot Market. While there were the usual vendors with tourist items and also artists and crafts people selling more expensive custom wares at the market, what was concerning was who and what was missing from the market. The lady selling lovely French linens that I so enjoy, the vendor selling many flavors of rum, all made on St. Maarten, and the spice man were absent from the Marigot Market. I hope they come back. The linens were so wonderful, the flavored rums were fun and bottled in beautiful and colorful artistic bottles, and I enjoyed purchasing gifts from the spice man. Other vendors I enjoyed were missing as well. Change had occurred in significant ways. Whether it will be permanent, we do not know.

And speaking of change, there were some positive changes at the market in the presence of new vendors. The market was smaller than in years past, but merchandise seemed plentiful. I am predicting that the market will continue to grow, and at some point, will return to its pre-Irma size. It is, after all, a part of the culture of St. Martin. In addition to the market conditions, many of the stores in Marigot were closed. Some had signs on them of dates when they would reopen, but others did not.

Mike and I went to Grand Case for lunch, in the past a wonderful area known across the Caribbean for its cuisine. We found only a couple of restaurants open and serving lunch. There was, however, a lot of rebuilding going on in this area. We settled on lunch at Fort Louis Yacht Club where we were kept company by several iguanas who are regular fixtures there.

Earlier in the week, Ron had invited us to his home for dinner for the first year anniversary of our time together braving the hurricane. It is special to be together with them at any time, but it was especially good to be together on this particular day. We enjoyed a delicious Indian meal and discussed our shared experience. In a positive change, Muskaan has a new business selling clothing and other items. She showed me some of her products, and I purchased a blouse. Sameer and Veer were typical children, playing with their technology and periodically engaging with us adults. It was a pleasant visit with friends with whom we are forever bonded.

Ron's soon to be two-and-a-half-year-old son, Veer

Mike and I drove back to our condo, very conscious of how different this day and evening with our friends had been compared to last year.

Thursday was The Day—the one year anniversary of Hurricane Irma coming to St. Maarten/St. Martin. Mike and I made our way to the Toppers Rhum Distillery to purchased our "Survivor Hurricane Irma September 2017" t-shirts. We wore them all day. We went to the local bookstore and purchased the *Discovery Irma* magazine and a #SXMStrong bracelet for each of us that contributed five dollars per bracelet to the hurricane recovery fund.

Mike and I wore our "Survivor Irma" t-shirts the whole anniversary day!

We talked to the woman at the bookstore about the "Irma" anniversary. She told us that there had been a two-minute prayer at the bank at 9:06 and that it was so touching that she cried. We asked her about any other ceremonies planned for the anniversary, and she said that she did not know of any. She did mention a local restaurant near the airport that was offering half-price drinks all day in honor of Irma survivors. Mike and I went to support the restaurant's efforts. In the local newspaper, there were several articles and proclamations from politicians about the anniversary. The articles referred to the day as a day of reflection. That did seem more appropriate than a day of celebration.

It was looking at the *Irma Discovery* magazine we

purchased that helped change my opinion of the island's clean up progress. The magazine had many photos of Irma's destruction. Looking at those photos, I no longer saw the destruction that is still present with the same eyes. I saw how much had been done, not how much still needed to be done. Given the lack of workers and money, what had been accomplished so far was amazing.

We went back to Toppers, the restaurant that produced and sold the Hurricane Irma Survivor t-shirts. We wanted to be there with others who might be wearing "Irma" t-shirts. The owner of Toppers was there and had an "Irma" t-shirt on. Coincidentally, Toppers was the last restaurant Mike and I went to right before settling in to weather Irma.

All in all, the anniversary day was a quiet and uneventful day. I had expected a celebration but decided that a quiet day of reflection was more appropriate and more than enough.

Friday was our last full day on the island. It had been a quick week. The traffic, however, was anything but quick that morning. We ended up going all around the island to get to Philipsburg. Mike commented that that was a way to see the entire island one last time on this trip.

We finally got to Philipsburg and started our time there at Joe's Jewelry profiling the staff on SAUCE, the profiling tool I use in my business. They wanted to retake the assessment to see if their data might have changed. Unfortunately, all of the previous reports were lost when the store's files and computers were destroyed by looters after Irma. I told them I would look for the originals in my files at home. When I gave them their results this time, Harry was sure that his data had changed significantly, and others thought they had some changes too. Everyone expressed the belief that the changes were due to the effects of Irma.

Later, conversation turned to a hurricane that is expected on St. Maarten in a few days, although it is not predicted to be as strong as Irma was. A different hurricane is expected in the Carolinas in the same time period. It is a given that this is hurricane season, but after Irma, I will never think of hurricanes or hurricane season as routine.

Saturday was our last day on St. Maarten. Before going to the airport, we rode to Maho one more time to see if we could find Nina, the Guest Relations Manager at the Royal Islander, as we had missed her each time we had stopped in. Although I was not hopeful that we would find her there this time since it was Saturday, we did. The three of us had a wonderful conversation. Her words were so inspiring that they will be the closing words of this part of the book.

We arrived at the airport three hours before our flight was scheduled to depart. Mike dropped me off to check-in and went to return the rental car. The process went smoothly, and I was already checked-in when Mike arrived from returning the rental car. His check-in went just as quickly, and we were in the waiting lounge with a couple of hours to spare before our plane was scheduled to depart.

It was very hot in the departure lounge, although there were large fans all around. Food and beverages were available to purchase as well as duty free items. There was even a temporary ice cream stand from the Carousel in Simpson Bay. Even though this temporary airport structure lacked the comfort and convenience of the permanent airport before Irma, it did not lack any of the services.

Our plane departed on schedule, delivering all of us from this lovely island to our various locations. As our plane lifted into the air, I felt sadness and relief. The sadness was due to leaving, although I am always glad to go home from a trip. The relief was from knowing that we would be back, that the island we love was rising again, and that although it would take some time, and there would be changes, it would return to its previous glory. It could even come through all this better and stronger! And so can we from our changes.

Post Script

These are the words of Nina Persaud, the Royal Islander's Guests Relations Manager, about St. Maarten/St. Martin.

> Something like this, Hurricane Irma, humbles you and changes your perspective on what's important. It makes you better, not bitter. You don't know what you are until you are tested. Your perspective changes. You are so much more than you were. It

takes a disaster to make us see what is really important. Life will never be the same for you, or for us, having been through this.

This is a small island with intention. We are not bitter at all. It is hope that sustains us more than anything else. What separates progress is effort. It changes your perspective on what's important. In tough times, you don't buckle.

We remain committed, more so than ever, to make sure that we hand over the keys in a better way than we found them. We are more than thankful to serve you. What you give to us is more than what we give to you. This is not a business for us. It is a community. As a famous man said, well, it was Jesus, "The greatest gift you can give to anyone is to serve."

PART III

The Lessons

Change Changes You

Paying Attention Helps You Make Better Decisions

Use All Experiences to Be Your Best Self

Change Changes You

Change is a fact of life, even unplanned and unwanted change. Some changes that occur for us are good changes, and some are not. Even so, in every change are lessons we can learn that will improve our lives. How we deal with change affects not just our own life, but the lives of those we care about.

The events I have written about in this book brought a

number of major changes for me. Most of the changes that have occurred and are still playing out this year were not changes I went looking for. A few changes had nothing to do with the events I've described here—they were just life moving on and shifting. It feels like most all of the significant changes this year, related or not to my key events, were unplanned and unwanted changes. Maybe this is because the events that brought them were not positive events. I would be unwise to assume perspective does not have some part to play in this evaluation!

What I can say is the events and resulting changes in my life taught or reminded me of valuable lessons—mostly, I would have to say, refresher lessons, so I can only conclude I must have needed to relearn them.

There are lessons in life that seem simple on the surface, even basic or trite, but the underlying truth is or at least can be—well, life changing. Every new experience, every encounter, every conversation, every action adds to or subtracts from who you are and how you perceive yourself. The change results are often mirrored back to you by those around you or at least create a reaction from those around you so in that sense the change ripples. These may be tiny changes but be assured even tiny changes build up. They form, compile, and become part of YOU by your actions and responses to them. Don't deny the power of cumulative, seemingly small, changes. Here's an example from my experience.

After three accidents in such a short period of time, I no longer take either driving or driving safely for granted.

First, it took me some time before I was ready to get back behind the steering wheel. The thought of driving—something that had been very second-nature to me—for a while seemed a dangerous endeavor to be avoided. That was a change. If I would have accepted that change, my ME would have become a very different person than my pre-accident me, and the course of my life would have made a very unwanted turn.

I worked on myself not to let this new fear define me, and I got myself back to driving. I rejected that change, or perhaps I should say I tamed it or remolded it. One way I did this was to choose a new vehicle with many built-in safety features. These safety features have been tools to help me rebuild my driving confidence. I can even say I am enjoying my new van because of these features. They make driving safely easier, and I am thankful for them, so the power of gratitude is now added to my change mix on driving. I just wish everyone could have vehicles with these wonderful, new safety features!

You can see from this example that when change appears, you may not have a choice about it showing up, but you do have choices or options within that change that will define or redefine you in a small or large way. As you also can see now, this is true even for events that come into your life that you may not think to define as change contributors—something like a vehicle accident. Everything creates change. It's up to you how you deal with these changes, significant or seemingly insignificant, as you are continually supporting/building your YOU.

Here's a larger change event. I no longer take life for granted in quite the same way as I did before Hurricane Irma. Yes, even after a frightening experience, a devastating loss, or a massive life-reshaping event, some level of normalcy or a new normal is achieved with time. In seismic positive changes—a big promotion, the birth of a child, the accomplishment of a highly desired goal—you also will find a new normal as that change sinks into your life. Regardless of the change agent, regardless of how the change is perceived, you never again are the same person you were before.

I thought there was a real possibility that I and others around me might die in this terrifying storm that was Irma and then—we didn't. We lived. I lived.

I know I am getting older. I know that I have fewer years in front of me than behind me. Mike and I have lost people dear to us in the past few years, some of whom I think I thought would live forever. Life is not the same without them. Their deaths changed our lives. But these painful losses were different than the immediacy of staring into a life-threatening situation during the storm.

I know—I really *do know*—so many other people face life-ending danger and threats whether due to natural disasters, war, poverty, repression, or the many other ills that beset our world, and those experiences are so horrifying, and I likely will never experience them. But still, the seven hours of being in the storm, feeling the possibility of death at our door, was for me, in my world, a life-altering experience.

A year later as I am finishing this book and after Mike and I went back to St. Maarten a year after the storm to see the place we love and to reconnect with the friends we have there, I have a new normal that is growing. I am changed. I did not brush off this event. I am working on how I continue to respond to the changes in me from all that last year brought.

I know Mike has changed too. Just not in the same way I have. He has just added one more adventure to his life story. Ron and his family, Harry, Joe's Jewelry, our staff friends at our own resort, and all the locals on St. Martin/ St. Maarten have had their own changes to shape their lives.

For me, I feel there is extra value for my days. I don't take any time I have for granted with the ease I did before. As I have been fortunate enough to push past my depression or unexpected PTSD symptoms, I relish the daily things life has in store and most certainly the time I can spend with Mike and our family and friends. While all of us know that we will not live forever, some days we act like we will. We do not pay enough attention to the fragility of life. I am *changing* that in my life, but to be honest, not enough, and not quickly enough.

Let's come back for a minute to dealing pragmatically with routine but uncontrollable change that occurs for all of us. We all have unplanned and unwanted changes such as those that come naturally with aging. Weight gain, hair loss, more aches and pains, and even more serious health concerns come to mind. Some of these require acceptance, for there is no turning back the aging clock. (I decided many years ago that I will not incur any intentional pain, so no tucks or lifts for me.) Sometimes we experience job loss, missed promotion opportunities, failure to be recognized for accomplishments, loss of a loved one, or housing or food scarcities for ourselves and our families. These things are change happening, and they will and do change us. The question is how change changes us—what effects change will produce.

I am not at all saying it is easy to deal with any kind of change. Some change is devastating. I'm not saying you or I or anyone can always deal with change on our own. What I am saying is that we must be aware that how we respond to change, especially unwanted, unwelcomed life-altering change, can/will change who we are and put us on a changed trajectory in life. I wish I could say just step up with a positive attitude and everything will be all right, but that would not always, or perhaps even not usually, be true. But what is true, is that working from the outside in or the inside out around change, taking whatever steps you can to make it into something workable will build a stronger you.

How do emotionally healthy people deal with unplanned and unwanted change? What resources can we use to help us get through those times? When dealing with any significant unwanted change, we first have to grieve. Dr. Elisabeth Kubler-Ross identified five stages of grief: denial, anger, bargaining, depression, and acceptance. Going through this process takes about a year for most people. Sometimes we need help through the journey.

Seek it through a counselor, coach, health care professional, or pastor/priest. Life will not be the same. We will not be quite the same. There is a good chance, however, that we will find happiness and joy again as we create a new normal with our actions and choices. My first lesson that I share with you, then, is that **change changes you.**

Paying Attention Helps You Make Better Decisions

Lack of Focus

The second lesson has to do with focus. Or perhaps I should say the lack of focus. Lack of focus results in us not paying attention, and when we fail to pay attention, we miss some things that can help us be safe, productive, and balanced. I have never been very good at focus. I am more driven to get things done quickly and so can end up making mistakes that can be costly and, at times, even dangerous. When hints of change start to come or when change drops in our lap—or on our head—being able to focus on what is happening is critical.

We can only get one thing at a time done well. I know we think we can multitask, and some of us spend a lot of time trying to accomplish that, thinking we are being more efficient. The reality is—and recent research proves—that we can only focus well on one thing at a time. Our brains are wired that way. When we try to multitask, we are not being as effective as we could be, and we are not even being efficient because our focus is diffused.

Personality is involved in handling change. Our natural tendencies—our normal reaction patterns—that are part of our personalities will come into play in dealing with change. This can be helpful or not helpful, which is where the focus comes in. We have to be aware of what is going on around us, and we need, especially in times of recognizable change, to understand that our natural tendencies will govern responses unless we consciously do something different. Understanding our own tendencies and using them effectively or moderating them when needed is important in dealing with change as it is happening and working with change in its aftermath. Likewise, and here is another important point, having some understanding about why someone else responds to the same change differently than we do can be helpful.

With regard to paying attention to and dealing with change, understanding things like where we are on a scale between fast action and focused planning or where we are between flexible and more linear or whether we put priority on people or results gives us understanding about our reactions to change and hopefully helps us better process what change brings. For example, while my personality is driven to fast action, Mike's is not—he is much more focused. We are a great team when we remember this and support each other to play to our individual strengths. We help each other avoid the mistakes that our natural tendencies can create.

Another personality aspect is the prominence of the flexible and friendly trait. As positive as these characteristics are, there is a downside. Conflict and confrontation are harder on people who are people-oriented and friendly. Since all change involves conflict, dealing with any conflict created when it isn't your natural skill set creates a different dynamic than for a person who isn't so close to your end of the scale.

There are many books about personality. The point here about personality is not to delve deeply as personality typing is not the purpose of this message. The point here is that recognizing that personality tendencies affect us as we deal with change can alert us that we may need to put additional skills we have into play. When we know, for example, that we are not naturally good in an area—let's say focus—then we know we may miss some details that can create problems for us. We may not be paying attention to some things that can help us, even keep us safe. We miss clues that could help us manage the change better. When we can call this to our own attention, we can more consciously learn to focus on focus! We can learn to pay better attention—and also to avoid unsafe or unwise distractions.

Distractions

Besides getting a new vehicle with built-in safety features, I have worked to change how I drive. I am more attentive to the road and other drivers than I was before the accidents. I no longer allow myself to be distracted when I drive. If I am being truthful, this is a work in progress.

All of us deal with distractions—some we can control

and some are difficult to control. No matter how they come, distractions reduce focus.

As I reflect on my car accidents, I do not recall being distracted by any specific thing or activity that could have contributed to those accidents, but I have to wonder if my attention was fully engaged in the task of driving. Was I thinking about work? Mentally making some kind of list? Or as a lovely old phrase goes, was I "wool gathering," letting my mind wander? There is current research about the magnitude of this problem. Being deep in thought about anything while driving, other than the driving itself, is very dangerous.

There are lots of poor driving habits that distract: using our mobile devices, combing our hair, putting on lipstick, and eating because we have not taken the time to stop for proper refreshment. Some people read while they are driving. I know this opinion of mine is not popular, but I do not understand how someone can be engrossed in an audio book and not be dangerously distracted. I love audio books while traveling as a passenger or when I am walking, doing house chores, or relaxing, but when I need to focus or concentrate, that is not the time for audio books for me. I suspect this would be true for many people.

My personal lesson from the accidents is that *consciously* driving safely is so important that I need to remove any distractions that prohibit me from totally focusing on the most important task while driving: keeping my eyes and mind on the road and other vehicles and nothing else!

Then there is the bigger distraction lesson from Hurricane Irma. We heard the official storm warnings. We saw posted notices. We heard and saw the concern of the locals. But we had had "mild" experiences from previous storms, we had a much-needed vacation mind-set, and the weather early in this period was beautiful. As I have already said, I have no idea why I, in particular, did not pay more attention. Maybe it was my optimistic nature, rose-colored glasses, or just head-in-the-sand syndrome until Mike and I both did take the coming storm seriously and, from that point, made focused decisions and prepared as best we could.

Discontinuities

I want to go back to a term I mentioned earlier: discontinuities. Paying attention to discontinuities is another way we can make better decisions. If you recall, discontinuities are described as things happening that just don't follow a logical pattern or that don't "fit." Some discontinuities are major indicators of change or impending change; others are not particularly important, although even those can provide us important and helpful information.

I can't really say discontinuity played a significant role in our storm experience, but it is such an important concept around change that it deserves a little attention here. I again use my life stories as examples.

As I think back on my life, I can recall several times that there were clear signs of something awry, things that did not fit, and I was either too busy and/or too stubborn to pay enough attention to them to figure out what they meant. Had I slowed down, paid attention to what was going on around me, and looked for other discontinuities to better understand what was happening, I could have been spared much pain.

Over time, I have learned that when things don't feel right or look right, they aren't right. Figuring out the pattern is where the real work begins. The small discontinuity I shared about my van rolling backwards when I was adjusting the position of the front tire by turning the steering wheel seemed so insignificant at the time that I really paid no attention and rushed to get to my meeting. Only later, after the first accident, did that discontinuity come to my mind again.

One example of clear discontinuity was missing the signs that I should have seen before the breakup of my first marriage. I completely missed those signs until I was hit over the head with information that was impossible to ignore. Another example is not recognizing the meaning of the discontinuities that occurred when I was a few months away from losing my executive job at Rex Hospital. After I was terminated, I could piece together discontinuities that had occurred while I was forging ahead, thinking I could "fix" things by continuing to do my job well. Had I paid attention, I would have recognized that I was being left out of meetings I should have been in, that my boss and I no longer had an easy and comfortable relationship, and that my position was in jeopardy.

Though at the time these things were occurring I did not know to call them discontinuities, I still should have been alert to the signs of change. Would I call this lack of attention? Would I call it misplaced focus? I'm not sure I know even now.

While you are reading this, you may have nagging thoughts about some discontinuities occurring in your own life. If so, spend some time trying to piece the quilt together, figuring out the pattern, and deciding how important, or not, the discontinuities are. Do not allow yourself to be in denial, thinking thoughts such as "it can never happen to me" or even going down the "what's happening isn't fair" path.

Change can and will happen to you, and it may be fair or not fair. The second lesson I am sharing with you is **paying attention helps you make better decisions**. Deal with whatever is happening head-on, teach yourself to pay attention, and practice focus so you can make the best decisions. Be proactive or you will be forced to be reactive. And we cannot make the best decisions from a position of reactivity.

Use All Experiences to Be Your Best Self

Mary Catherine Bateson, cultural anthropologist and writer, is known for her saying about our lives being like a tapestry made up of our different experiences and that sometimes it takes years for us to figure out the pattern. I interpret this to mean that all of our experiences provide meaning to our lives, even those, and maybe even *especially* those, that are most painful. In those experiences, we can find lessons. If we pay attention and deal with change facing forward and learn from our experiences, we can work through change. We build a new normal constantly in little ways and big. Today might be similar to, better than, or not as good as yesterday. Our reactions to change, even our awareness of change, become part of us and thus part of our lives. We can do better. We can do worse. We can do something differently. We can learn from mistakes. We can learn new, wonderful things. All from change.

Elisabeth Kubler-Ross, the author of several wonderful books and the one who developed the stages of grief that I referenced earlier in this book, also wrote about learning from our experiences. Her philosophy was that there are no accidents in our lives, that all things happen for a reason, and it is incumbent on us to figure out the reasons for what happens. I do not think this means that we are helpless to chart our own course, that what happens to us is predestined. I interpret this to mean that all of our experiences provide meaning to our lives, and, in a similar way to what Mary Catherine Bateson said, we need to figure out the pattern.

I certainly can look back on my life and see the patterns and believe the magic of my life is all of my experiences. In every trauma, there was also joy. In every disappointment, there was a lesson. In every event, there was a part of the pattern that propelled me forward and helped me grow or stopped me in my tracks and kept me from growing until I learned the lessons the experience was sent to teach me.

The experiences of 2017 temporarily stopped me in my tracks until I learned the lessons I was meant to learn, changing me from the inside out. My third lesson to you is to **use all your experiences to become your best self**.

PART IV

CHANGE AND BEHAFIOR

Change and Behavior

One of the most significant lessons from Hurricane Irma was the fragility of life. There are likely only a few times in our lives we experience really life-changing events. When faced with a major crisis such as a category 5 hurricane making a direct hit where life and property are in jeopardy, our life changes on a dime. When something is totally out of our control, all of our internal resources are affected. We have the choice to close down and become immobilized or meet the crisis with all of our internal resources.

The "choice" may not be conscious or intentional. We may be in a "fight or flight" response. How we have behaved in other traumatic situations conditions us to what our behavior will be in a current or future crisis. While fear is involved, the impact of the fear will vary from individual to individual.

People who deal best with fear and change that are outside of their control have a healthy self-esteem, are typically confident and competent, and are assertive. It is certainly true that at times in our lives we possess different degrees of each of these.

The happiest and most effective people bounce back quicker from situations that can negatively impact confidence and competence than those who routinely struggle to be effective or to find happiness in their lives. Personality traits are also variables that have significant impact on our behavior.

There are four types of behavior; ***non-assertive***, ***assertive***, ***aggressive***, and ***passive aggressive***. Each type of behavior includes verbal and non-verbal components. While in general, assertive behavior is best in most situations, there are times in which exercising non-assertive or aggressive behavior may be warranted. I do not think the same is true for passive aggressive behavior.

Non-assertive behavior basically can be described as failure to verbalize and/or show what one really thinks and feels. Its expression includes not making good eye contact, voice too soft, stooped shoulders, and fidgeting. People who are non-assertive rarely achieve what they are capable of achieving. They are often too concerned about the opinion of others. Non-assertive people are often perceived by others as lacking confidence.

Assertive behavior is an honest statement of feelings and thoughts, use of objective words, and a general assured manner. The tone of voice is firm yet warm and relaxed, eye contact is open and direct without staring, and posture is well-balanced. Most situations are best managed with assertive behavior. People who regularly exhibit assertive behavior are usually perceived by others as confident and competent.

Aggressive behavior is extreme behavior including subjective and inflammatory words, an exaggerated show of strength, and an inflated sense of self. The voice is loud, demanding, and authoritarian. Eye contact is cold and staring. Body posture is overbearing. People who exhibit aggressive behavior have difficulty getting along with other people and often are perceived by others as arrogant.

Passive aggressive behavior can be one of two types. The first type is displayed by the person who is often non-assertive, who at some point has taken and taken and taken and then whose behavior becomes aggressive with pent up emotion that may explode. The second type of passive aggressive behavior is divisive in nature exhibited by the person who goes behind the backs of others. This person is often untrustworthy.

As this book is part of my attempt to process my 2017 experiences, including my fears, and to learn what I needed to learn from the changes that came in my life, I know I need to assess my perspectives and my lessons through my own strengths and weaknesses. It seemed to me, then, that readers might find it interesting to complete some assessments that will point to a few of their own traits, so I have included some very simple tools as Appendices in this book.

The purpose of these tools is not an in-depth personality analysis or any sort of diagnostic. These are more awareness tools, but the insight they offer can help you manage change more effectively by understanding how you are likely to process it. These assessment tools can help identify strengths and areas of needed improvement related to behavior and change.

Since self-confidence and self-esteem are both involved in dealing with change effectively, it is helpful to understand a bit more clearly the difference between these two attributes and reflect on your own level of strength or weakness with each. While the terms self-esteem and self-confidence are sometimes used interchangeably, they are not the same. A comparison of these attributes can be found in Appendix I, as well as notes on their relationship to change.

Appendix II is a Confidence and Competence assessment tool related to understanding your most important needs. Needs are different than wants. We are not able to feel confident and be competent when we do not get our most important needs met. Appendix II also addresses the relationship of confidence and competence to dealing with change.

Appendix III is my Assertiveness Quotient Assessment tool. Answers to the questions on this tool help to evaluate how assertive, or not, you are, and in which situations you tend to be more or less assertive. People who are more confident, competent, and assertive deal with unplanned and unwanted change easier and better than people who have challenges in these areas.

I encourage you to use these three simple tools to help you manage change that comes into your life more effectively by understanding how you are likely to process it when it arrives—because it will arrive! For those who may be interested, you can find out more about the SAUCE Personality Assessment that I spoke of using at Joe's Jewelry at https://www.fralixgroup.com/resources.

My Wish for You

Whether you choose to use the assessment tools or not, I hope reading about the ordinary and extraordinary events in my life in 2017 as change agents and my reflections on them will help you think about change in your life. Maybe to create a little more focus or awareness. Maybe to think about how YOU work with change. If you care to share your story of change with me, you can reach me at ***https://www.fralixgroup.com/contact-us***. In the meantime, I wish you fair weather and good change.

Appendix I

Self-Esteem and Self-Confidence

The terms Self-Esteem and Self-Confidence are often used interchangeably. This is incorrect. The table below identifies the differences in these.

Self-Esteem…

- Belief in yourself at the core
- Believe you are a person of worth, deserving of the best from yourself and others
- Healthy self-esteem comes from positive nurturing as a child

Self-Confidence…

- Belief in one's knowledge and ability to perform effectively
- Changes when one is in new and/or challenging situation
- Comes from successful achievement

Relationship to Change

People who struggle with issues of self-esteem and/or self-confidence have more difficulty dealing with change than those who have healthy self-esteem and self-confidence. This is especially true when the change is perceived to be or is outside of one's control. There are decisions we can make to improve our self-confidence and self-esteem.

Self-confidence is the easier of the two to improve. Our self-confidence comes from our feelings of being successful and achieving what is important to us. If we lack self-confidence, we can:

- make sure that we spend the majority of our time with people who value us.

- continue to upgrade our skills, knowledge, experience, and our education. Education does not need to be just formal education. It can be self-learning, including reading, listening to podcasts and other audio resources, and continuing education classes and activities.

- focus on our strengths more than trying to improve our weaknesses.

- be in a career and job that inspires us and makes us feel competent.

- remove people, activities, and jobs from our lives that do not help us grow and improve.

- have a coach who can help us grow and develop ourselves into our best self.

If we lack self-esteem, this is more difficult to change, but change is certainly possible. Issues of self-esteem usually require the help of a therapist or other professional. It is usually not sufficient to try to solve these issues alone or even with the support of strong relationships. Individuals who have a trusting relationship with a good therapist are best able, over time, to develop healthy self-esteem.

Additionally, the suggestions for dealing with self-confidence should also be used to deal with self-esteem. Also, many people report that meditation and yoga are effective in improving overall well-being,

Appendix II

Confidence and Competence Assessment

Rank the following four choices as most true to least true with (1) being most true and (4) being least true for you.

I feel best about myself (confident) and am most effective (competent) when I:

_____ am able to act quickly.

_____ have order and stability.

_____ have the validation or approval of others.

_____ am involved and understood.

The response you have ranked as (1) is your greatest need. This is a true need, not a want, for you to find your greatest success. You will not be able to be confident or competent without this occurring.

Key to Understanding the Confident and Competent Need Levels with Regard to Dealing with Change

General information about your (1), (2), (3), and (4) rankings.

First, it is most important to understand your #1 answer. If your #1 answer is A (am able to act quickly), you need to be able to get things done without interference or being controlled by others and to do so within your chosen time frame. If you are not able to do so, you are not able to be your best self. During times of change you may act impulsively and become controlling of others.

If your #1 answer is B (have order and stability), unplanned change, especially change that happens quickly, adversely impacts your confidence and competence. You need time to adjust to change, and when you do not have that time, you cannot be your best self.

If your #1 answer is C (have the validation or approval of others), you need the validation or approval of others to be your best. If you lack this, you are not as confident and competent as you can be when this external validation or approval is present. Of these two, "validation and approval," the one most problematic is "approval." It is easier to get validation than approval. If the need is for approval, in a rapidly changing world with competition between people often present, the need for someone else's approval leaves one very vulnerable.

If your #1 answer is D (am involved and understood), when you feel left out of decisions or when you feel that others do not understand you—which is different than others not agreeing with you—you cannot be your best self. Instead of feeling confident and competent and displaying those behaviors to others, too often you sound argumentative to others. You can make assumptions and personalize things to the point that the relationships with others worsen. When you are not involved in changes that affect you, and/or when you do not feel understood during those changes, you can become argumentative and controlling and not operate within boundaries.

After understanding your #1 answer, it is easiest to then understand your #4 answer. Your #4 answer is the one that is not a need for you, and likely not even a want. You can lack this and it will not affect your confidence or competence.

Then look at your #2 answer. This is also a need for you, not just a want. You need to have this to be confident and competent. In times of rapid change, and especially changes that you question or disagree with, it is important to take ownership of doing whatever you can to get your #1 and #2 needs met.

Your #3 answer is probably more of a want than a need. You can be confident and competent without it.

Although your #1 and #2 answers are more needs than wants, in times of major change that is happening quickly, you will be more confident and competent when you have all four levels met to some degree. The degree to which these are more or less important is found in the ranking order.

Appendix III

Assertiveness Quotient (AQ)

Indicate how often you are assertive in each of the following by circling the number most representative of your behavior:

1. Never 2. Rarely 3. Sometimes 4. Usually 5. Always

1. When a person is blatantly unfair, do you say something about it to her? *1 2 3 4 5*

2. Do you say what you think and/or feel, even at the risk of a conflict with others? *1 2 3 4 5*

3. Do you involve yourself socially without fear of doing or saying the wrong thing? *1 2 3 4 5*

4. If someone betrays your confidence, do you tell him how you really feel? *1 2 3 4 5*

5. If your manager asked you to work overtime when it was inconvenient, would you tell her? *1 2 3 4 5*

6. When a clerk in a store waits on someone who has come in after you, do you call the clerk's attention to the matter? *1 2 3 4 5*

7. Are you willing to ask a good friend to lend you a few dollars? *1 2 3 4 5*

8. Do you ask others for help when you need it? *1 2 3 4 5*

9. If a co-worker wants to chat when you would rather be working, do you tell him so? *1 2 3 4 5*

10. If a person teases you, do you tell them what you think or feel? *1 2 3 4 5*

11. When you enter a crowded auditorium, do you look for a seat up front rather than stand in the rear? *1 2 3 4 5*

12. If someone keeps kicking the back of your seat in a movie, would you ask her to stop? *1 2 3 4 5*

13. Do you confront co-workers when they don't do their share, rather than just "grin and bear it?" *1 2 3 4 5*

14. If someone starts talking to someone else in the middle of your conversation, do you express your displeasure? *1 2 3 4 5*

15. In a restaurant, if you order a medium steak and find it too rare, would you ask the server to have it re-cooked? *1 2 3 4 5*

16. Do you challenge work that you think is inappropriate or unfair? *1 2 3 4 5*

17. Would you return a faulty garment you purchased a few days ago? *1 2 3 4 5*

18. If someone you respect expresses opinions with which you strongly disagree, would you express your own point of view? *1 2 3 4 5*

19. When a close friend calls you on the phone, and you prefer to not talk, do you say so? *1 2 3 4 5*

20. Would you remind your manager of an overdue raise? *1 2 3 4 5*

Scoring: Assertiveness Quotient (AQ)

Calculate the score by adding the numbers for questions 1-20 above for the individual's AQ: _________

Locate the individual's AQ on the scale below:

20	**40**	**60**	**80**	**100**
Never	**Rarely**	**Sometimes**	**Usually**	**Always**

Adapted from the *Assertiveness Quotient*
by George R. Warsaw and Richard Blue

People who are assertive are best able to get their own needs met, yet not alienate others while doing so. They work well with others to accomplish results. The behavior that is most effective in most situations is assertiveness. Were it only this simple, however, we would not have as many challenges in getting along well with others while accomplishing our own results!

In times of change, especially change that is unplanned and that happens quickly, one's strength can become a weakness. For example, assertiveness can become aggressiveness. Also, the other person's personality must be considered, not just one's own. For example, assertive behavior can feel like aggressive behavior to a nonassertive person, and it can feel like nonassertive behavior to an aggressive person.

This Assertiveness Quotient is intended to help you assess your assertiveness tendencies in general as well as in different situations.

Once you have answered the questions and calculated your score, interpret your score as follows:

If your score is 60 or above, consider your assertiveness to be above average. The higher the score the more assertive you are. If your score is too high, however, you may be too assertive, even aggressive!

Then look at the questions in detail to determine if you are more or less assertive in different situations. For example, you may be more assertive when dealing with people you know, yet less assertive when dealing with a boss, or vice versa. In this analysis, interpret your score of 3 or above as assertive, and below 3 as less assertive on these individual questions.

Given your overall score and your score in the individual answers, decide where your strengths are related to assertiveness and where your opportunity areas are.

Recognize that in times of major change, especially unplanned change and change outside of your control, you will fare best if you are assertive. If you lack assertiveness during these times, expect that you will not be able to have or achieve what is in your best interest.

About the Author

Patti Fralix is an author, speaker, consultant, and coach plus a wife, mother to two daughters, and grandmother to three granddaughters and a grandson, all of whom are the lights of her life. She is known for regularly hosting seated dinner parties for more than 40 people, is on the go traveling for her business and with her husband, and has a deep and abiding love for beautiful (but not necessarily expensive) things, satisfied in part by her small antiques business. Her life is full of (mostly) controlled mess, stress, and less!

Patti began her career in the health care industry as a nurse and then a hospital executive. After a seismic event, she found her best self and became founder and president of The Fralix Group, Inc. Her unique ability to connect with clients and audiences through real life experience, hers and others, creates effective, dynamic connections and results in her work. Whether the setting is a management or staff retreat, a team building session, or a convention and whether the topic is Leadership, Teamwork, or Customer Service, Patti encourages and inspires each person to achieve individual and organizational results by being their best selves. Comments audience participants and clients consistently use for Patti include: "Inspiring," "Engaging," "Challenging," "Practical," and "Entertaining." ***www.fralixgroup.com***

www.ingramcontent.com/pod-product-compliance
Lightning Source LLC
LaVergne TN
LVHW051248080426
835513LV00016B/1802

* 9 7 8 1 9 4 6 4 2 5 3 5 5 *